Getting the Word Out

FREDERICK H. GONNERMAN

Getting the Word Out

The Alban Guide to Church Communications

The Alban Institute

Library of Congress Catalog Number 2003105601
ISBN 1-56699-283-4

07   06   05   04   03   VG   1   2   3   4   5   6   7   8   9   10

Contents

Foreword

Fred Gonnerman has written a frank, delicious, unshamefaced, and helpful "how to" book. Turn your search engine on the Web loose to scan "books in print," and take note of just a few that might interest you. Some will appeal to readers who have specialties that are too remote to hold your interest. Others are of little help to anyone. *Getting the Word Out* should be among the surviving titles on your list—a genuinely helpful volume.

Early on, Gonnerman clears his throat and apologizes for his necessary use of the word *competition* in the field of communication for the church. He knows that word is borrowed from free enterprise economics, where it can reflect not only initiative and freedom but also ruthlessness and the "doing in" of a rival. He knows that, even worse, in the Christian community, competition can refer to efforts to seduce members of other congregations or communions and get them to join one's own. Further, competition can mean lining things up in order to achieve enough for a church to boast about, and we all know what the apostle Paul had to say about boasting in the kingdom and the church.

So by making clear what competition means here, Gonnerman begins to develop the thesis of his book. Think of competition not as working against other Christians but competing against one's self, one's own present products. Gonnerman could remind us that half the American people may have "preferences" but make no "commitments." When church communications are designed to help draw in people who are not yet part of a congregation, those communications can draw people to make commitments.

Gonnerman realistically admits that church communications have to compete for the time, attention, investment, and priorities of those who might receive, contribute to, or in some other way respond to them. What Gonnerman is after is that his readers first appraise how they have communicated and then to engage in self-criticism. He shows us how to do those things. Next he encourages us to develop the skill to do better—and he again shows how to do it. And finally, he teaches us how to present a new product.

Gonnerman mentions that in his workshops, he is sometimes accused of making people squirm. Still, he has a gentle hand, is positive in his intent, and is not given to deep irony or savage sarcasm. In fact, I think that he includes many examples of bad communication that would have invited satire from less generous souls. Among them would be the author of this foreword who, for four decades, has written frequent columns taking off from typographical errors, infelicities, and howlers in church papers and bulletins. But if people do squirm, they will do so because Gonnerman's discernments are telling. No doubt the biblical prophets also made people squirm!

In fact, if one can squirm retroactively for past faults and failures, count me in the company. I was a parish pastor for a decade, long enough ago that the statute of moral and aesthetic limitations has run out on me. During that time I think I committed all the sins and made all the errors to which Gonnerman points in this book. And I did all that in a simple world where print communications in a congregation relied on typing and mimeographing. He threads us through a much more complex technological maze, where one can more frequently get lost, bump into walls, or explode in fury.

If I reread my own little church newsletter editorials of decades ago, I would find them on the front page, where pastor's columns, I learn too late, do not belong. A pastor who does not learn to bring forth talent from staff and lay members, many of whom have gifts and impulses to write, usually bangs out something because there is space saved for her or him: "Hey, Pastor, I *need* those 550 words first thing tomorrow; the mailing is due in the afternoon."

When I have glanced back at them, I have been embarrassed to find that I often then did what I later criticized: I wrote what I call "lettuce" columns. Weary from calling, administering, studying, preparing sermons, I dashed off something with a hortatory conclusion that began, "Therefore, let us . . ." Scientific surveys would suggest that in all history no one has been swayed by such a "lettuce" column. People are swayed when, as Gonnerman shows, church communicators have learned to compete for attention and found the right to command it; when they see themselves as part of the church's story and not as customers or people to be cajoled; and when they know that those who are communicating have first listened to them, and responded with something to say.

This book shows how to involve more than a pastor and one assistant in print (and sometimes electronic) communications. It is a book whose author remembers the communion of saints, the priesthood of all believers, the ministry of all the baptized, the variety of gifts that represent the one Spirit in the body of Christ.

To his credit and our benefit, the author takes church publications seriously. They represent an undervalued and overlooked form of communication. No doubt more people use Sunday church bulletins than read daily newspapers. Paul Westermeyer, professor of worship at Luther Seminary in St. Paul, in one of his books on congregational singing, startled readers by reminding them that every weekend nearly fifty million adult Americans sing together. He was not thinking of their humming and mumbling during the National Anthem at athletic events; he meant in church. With that constituency, he made the case—the church must do its best. So it is with church communications. They represent the Word of God, the work of the church, the aspiration to enlarge the scope of human service and, if miracles are allowed to happen, they may even delight the readers who are beckoned by them.

Martin E. Marty

Preface

Welcome to the intriguing world of faith-related public relations and publications. It is a world whose dimensions have been changing rapidly with each passing decade; a world that came into being when Johann Gutenberg, the "father of printing," began using movable type in the mid-15th century in Germany. More recently, publication in congregations has moved quickly from manual typewriters and duplicating machines to electric typewriters and mimeographs to word processors and copying machines to e-mail and Web pages.

Getting the Word Out: The Alban Guide to Church Communications is written for two related audiences. First, the book is for pastors, priests, rabbis, and other spiritual leaders who have taken on the tasks of congregational public relations and publications. Some see such work as no more or less than an unpleasant chore that takes up far too much time, but has to be done on a weekly and monthly basis. Others see their efforts in congregational public relations and publication as an integral part of their multi-tasked ministries, yet something that requires expertise they know they don't have.

Second, the book is for the laypersons—secretaries and administrative assistants and volunteer or appointed editors—who have the tasks involved in parish publications and public relations as an integral part of their job descriptions. But they seldom have the time to sit back and look creatively at why the congregation does these things and what might be done to make the results more effective.

Getting the Word Out is a systematic look at what needs to be done from a public relations and publications standpoint to be most helpful to a congregation's ministry. It starts with becoming aware of the competition, the purposes of a publications program, and systematic audience analysis. Then the book moves to making words and formats readable. Two chapters offer ideas for the creative content of newsletters and worship service guides and how that material can be organized to be most useful to the reader. The combination of responsibility and authority is discussed. Relationships with the public media, use of photography, and opportunities for electronic ministry are parts of the mix. One chapter deals with the role of publications in the celebration of special events; and in every instance, the book provides help in how to do it.

This book makes frequent forays into the connections between a congregation's publications and public relations program, and the effectiveness of its efforts in promoting better stewardship, giving emphasis to effective evangelism, and working out the elements of exciting parish education. In other words, *Getting the Word Out* contends that a congregation's ministries in stewardship, evangelism, and education are enhanced substantially by a public relations and publications ministry that borrows unashamedly from the experience and expertise of professional journalists, graphic designers and artists, photographers, and public relations personnel.

Good congregational public relations is a team effort. Ideally, depending on the size of the congregation or its budget, the communications and public relations team includes the pastor, a volunteer or paid editor, the congregation secretary, other paid staff, and the lay leadership of the congregation. *Getting the Word Out* is written to help every member of the team understand the need to assist and support the editor in efforts to produce the most effective and highest quality publications possible.

I must express my appreciation to the hundreds of workshop participants I have worked with over the past four decades for their assistance in helping me frame workable solutions to the problems inherent in parish public relations programs. The thousands of bulletins and newsletters I have read and critiqued over those years have provided graphic illustration of both good and not so good modes and methods of congregational communication.

The illustrations used in this book have been culled from hundreds of examples and are printed as much as possible as they originally appeared in line length, typeface, and typesize. Only the names have been changed to protect both the innocent and the guilty. I hope you find the suggested rewrites useful. Keep in mind that the rewrite you see is only one of several ways the communications problems in the original might be solved. Language is too alive and vibrant to be locked into only one form of expression.

Enjoy *Getting the Word Out.* Put it to use where and as you can.

1

The Competition Factor

Many faith group members and leaders continue to think that *competition* is an ecclesiastically dirty word. The competition concept gets hooked up tightly with proselytizing; thankfully, that has not been in vogue in mainline congregations for a long time. Apart from a few groups at the core of fundamentalism, congregations today do not intentionally climb fences into another congregation's sheepfold to entice away any of the lambs that might be restless there.

Contemporary congregations strive to produce parish publications—particularly newsletters and worship service guides—that will help them to be competitive for the time and minds of their own members, as well as their potential unchurched prospects. Consider the periodic newsletter, that too-often innocuous publication carried by postal carriers to the mailboxes of nearly every member of congregations at least once a month. When it arrives near the end of the month with its announcements of all the good things that are going to be happening in a congregation for the next 30 to 45 days, it most often arrives in a very competitive environment.

Analyzing the Competition in the Mailbox

First, the newsletter must compete with all the other mail for that day. In most households, that probably includes at least one catalog, a couple of bills, an invitation or two to contribute some charitable dollars to a worthy cause in addition to the faith group, invitations to subscribe to yet another publication, a news magazine, and a special interest magazine or two.

If you live in a small town or rural community, your mail might also include the local weekly newspaper. And in amongst all those carefully researched, professionally written and designed, full-color, glossy publications hides your congregation's newsletter.

What is the householder going to read first? And if your congregation's newsletter is laid aside for later reference, how soon, if ever, will that person get back to read, digest, and be motivated by the information?

In too many cases, parish publication editors are still trying to attract attention to their newsletters by overusing clip art, printing the text in old-fashioned typewriter-style typefaces, and squeezing everything together in a format that is, at best, chaotic. (Each of these problems is discussed later, particularly in chapter 5.) The content is verbose, with its emphasis deep in the past and often inconsequential to the reader's life and activity schedule (or at least, it's perceived that way). Add to that the problematic low-quality reproduction of a copy machine low on toner, and that newsletter is in big trouble. Competitively, it does not stand much of a chance except from the congregation's most dependable readers.

The newsletter is the congregation's one shot at reaching 100 percent of the membership every month. After all, on average, only about 30 percent of the members can be expected to be in the sanctuary for any scheduled worship service. To complicate the picture, the competition for reading time for your congregation's monthly newsletter goes far beyond the material in your mailbox on the day (or the week) it arrives.

The Lifestyle-Driven Competition for Time

In many families today, both spouses are employed outside the home. They both come home tired, one of them prepares dinner, the other does some of the ever-present chores that pervade a household, and the children attending school need help with their homework as well as taxi service to all the after-school activities.

After all of that, maybe a little time is left over to watch a favorite TV program before everyone is so tired they have to go to bed. The whole cycle starts again early the next morning with a rushed breakfast, and parents and children all going off in separate directions. Somehow, in all that, reading the congregation's newsletter does not get high priority. And if it isn't read the day it arrives, the chances that it will be read at all diminish substantially with every passing day thereafter. Unless, of course, the people involved already happen to be active in their congregation and have already marked it as a priority in their lives. But that is a bit like "preaching to the choir." Those people are also already part of the 30 percent who are in the sanctuary every worship day.

Worship Service Folder Competition: A Matter of Impressions

Even the worship service folder seen regularly by that 30 percent of the membership, as well as the occasional visitors, needs a competitive edge.

The programs your members receive at cultural events, the printed guides at artistic and historical exhibits, the materials handed out at flower and auto shows are filled with information presented in attractive, readable formats. The promotional pieces they pick up at auto dealers, farm implement shops, appliance stores, and the state fair are most often multicolored, market-tested publications that attract readership and leave an impression of quality.

Few congregations have budgets that allow for such sophisticated printing of their worship service folders, and even if they did, they probably would not choose to spend it there. They do, however, need to pay attention to writing those worship service folders in clear, concise, and objective language that is organized systematically (see chapter 4). And from a competitive standpoint, it is also important that the information in the worship service folder be printed in readable typefaces and presented in creative formats (see chapter 5).

The competition factor between worship service guides and promotional brochures is not a side-by-side comparison about which one gets read first. It is, instead, a competition of impressions, a subtle comparison with other publications suggesting that the congregation cares as much about the content and quality of the presentation of its message as commercial organizations care about theirs. And parishioners are pleased when they can see that the ministry of their congregation includes the budgeting of adequate time and money to ensure that the bulletin it prints provides the highest possible quality of communication for all the members and visitors who use it to assist them in worship.

That competitive quality is evident in several relatively simple ways. The guide to worship is clear and instructive. Worshipers are made to feel welcome. Notes of appreciation are free of clichés. The announcements work in tandem with the larger stories already printed in the newsletter. The congregation and its leaders are appropriately identified. The layout and design are visually attractive.

Responding to People's Perceptions

The perceptions of people are as important as their knowledge of specific facts, and alert congregations are aware of the distinctions, because facts and perceptions are not always the same.

Even though costs of sophisticated publication have gone down substantially in recent years, and even if a congregation has all the money it needs to invest in publication development and production, it might not be wise to produce parish publications that some would look at as too slick or too sophisticated and, consequently, as too expensive.

In the eyes of some parishioners, such expenditures are not good stewardship of the faith group's finances even though an improved newsletter has the potential to strengthen the congregation's ministry and substantially increase regular attendance at worship services. If that's the case in your congregation, some special education is needed for the financially conservative members regarding communication and communication needs.

Fine lines of distinction divide extravagant from elaborate from sophisticated, expensive from fancy, ordinary from mundane. Sadly, if potential readers of a congregation's newsletter think that a publication is extravagant, it does not matter whether it actually is extravagant or not. Even though the costs of multicolored printing on better quality papers have decreased substantially in recent decades, the perception that a newsletter or a worship service guide is too expensive is probably too costly for a congregation's internal goodwill. Lesser misconceptions have driven deep wedges of conflict into more than one congregation through the years.

The congregation needs to change negative perceptions based on wrong impressions to appreciation based on the substance, timeliness, attractiveness, and economy of its publications program. If negative perceptions seem to be a problem, perhaps when the annual budget is proposed to the congregation, a brief education program is in order to point out the actual costs of the communications bargain their offerings are helping to pay for. As a congregation plans improvements in the quality of a publication, the reasons, expectations, and intentions of those improvements should be explained clearly. The related changes in costs can also be spelled out objectively and in detail even before members of the congregation see the first changes.

Full-color printing is not a likely option for all but a few congregations. Even then, such sophistication would probably not be sound stewardship of a congregation's resources. Two-color printing, on the other hand, is quite achievable, at least on the four sides of any cover (front, back, inside front, and inside back) that folds around the inside content. Creative use of two-color printing (or copying) often gives the impression that even more than two colors are being used. If the budget does not allow more than a two-color cover, one-color printing with imaginative graphics can communicate—and compete—well on the inside pages. One-color printing does not have to be staid and sterile. Black ink on white paper is always safe. But dark brown, dark blue, or burgundy ink on earth tone papers can be just as readable and usually is a more interesting option.

A typeface that is contemporary, serif (more is said about that in chapter 5), and large enough to read easily in lines that can be comprehended quickly will automatically make any publication more appealing. And the typefaces in any given publication are limited to no more than three (two is even better) in spite of the fact that your computer has hundreds of fonts to play with. Forget most of them. Only a handful is close to readable. Layout needs symmetry and cohesion. It is designed in patterns that are predictable and can be depended upon for consistency by readers as they turn from page to page.

Emphasizing Substantive Content

Most important, the competitive newsletter and worship service guide are filled with content that focuses on substance. When readers give your congregation's newsletter 15 minutes of their time, they expect the publication to amplify the mission of the congregation which is (or might become) their home.

Even more important, the newsletter motivates all its readers to become an active part of the ministries that are going on in their congregation. They know that the moments they take to read their congregation's newsletter are a valuable stewardship of their limited time. They also know that their parish newsletter will challenge them to respond actively to their God-given faith. At the same time, prospective members are attracted through the newsletter to give serious consideration to active membership in a congregation where they have already indicated interest. And that happens because the monthly parish newsletter, as it announces opportunities for worship, education, and service, gives form and substance to the revelation of God's power at work in your congregation.

The major reason you strive to make your parish newsletters and your worship service guides competitive publications is that they are some of your major tools of evangelism, stewardship, education, and service, all primary supporting pillars of an active, lively congregation.

In reality, parish publications are only one part of the competition challenge. Every congregation knows it is competing for the time, talent, and energies of all of its members. As worship service folders and periodic newsletters tell the story of what a congregation's life and ministry is about, they also inform the life of the members to help them feel called to daily discipleship while challenging them to accept a more active role in their congregation's life and leadership.

Well-informed members are men, women, and youth who are moved by the competitive quality and content of their parish's publications. They take the time to read those publications and keep themselves informed about the congregation's mission, and they are much more likely to carve out the time in which they will use their energy and talents in service to the God of their faith and life. They are the ones who are already busy in their call to personal ministry as hardworking and trusted employees or employers, faithful spouses and parents, and caring members of their neighborhoods and school communities. They are also the ones who can be depended upon to respond to their own as well as the congregation's need to serve and lead on councils and committees, teach the congregation's children, youth, and adults on a weekly basis, and serve in special lay ministries.

They will also be more likely to have a stronger giving record. The more that people know about the work of a congregation, the more they are challenged to become an evermore active part of the life of that same congregation, and the more eager they are to invest in making the total ministry of this people more effective. A major part of that assistance is giving a proportionate—even a sacrificial—share of their financial resources to make sure that the ministry of their congregation is always reaching out and never in danger of being cut back. That kind of stewardship is a bright reflection of both their personal and their corporate faith.

Your parish communications, written and designed to be competitive, and the general public relations ministry of your congregation, sensitive and responsive to the needs and concerns of all its audiences, can be a major force in helping to make that happen.

2

Why Do All This Work, Anyway?

No matter whether they are worship service guides, periodic newsletters, or some special printed program, parish publications are a lot of work. Why bother? What is their purpose? What is their effect?

Some congregations seldom ask those questions. When they do, the answer is too often a version of, "We've always done that." A review of purposes and effects is always in order. In fact, it is good practice for a congregation to conduct a review of its total publications and public relations program once every year.

The review starts with a meeting of the pastor and the office staff, but it is wise to move beyond that group to include the public relations committee (see chapter 8), a few active members of the congregation who are not currently in leadership roles. Results of the review should be reported to the council or board for its input and approval.

Only with such an annual review will a congregation's publications be kept fresh, lively, and the effective tools of communication they are intended to be. See appendix A for an outline that will help your congregation review and audit its own publications and public relations programs. Once the practice of annual reviews begins, always check information in the previous year's review with the current review to see what changes have been made and whether they have had the intended effect.

So what should the purposes of parish publications be? Try these four.

- To inform
- To educate
- To motivate
- To edify

Let's examine each of those purposes one at a time.

To Inform

Communicating the substantive stuff of worship, study, stewardship, evangelism, education, and other opportunities for active involvement and personal piety is a critical component of every congregation's ministry. That's the who, what, when, where, and why or how of what's going on in the parish. To be most effective, the preponderant emphasis of that information focuses on the future: What is going to be happening? Who is going to be involved? What meaning will it have for the life of the congregation and the faith of its members?

But what do people need to be informed about? Put most simply, members need to know the congregation's mission and the programs the faith group creates to make that mission work. Information confirms why a congregation exists, and how it communicates that ongoing mission to its members, its prospective members, and its community. An announcement that a group is going to meet again for its regular monthly meeting on the same day at the same time in the same place as it does every month is not particularly exciting information. More important, that kind of "news" is not going to motivate participation by people on the inactive roster or those who are not yet members.

Consider, however, an announcement to that same group that focuses on a special program, designed creatively, with an eye to its appeal for those people who are not members as well as those who are. Now, *that* information is important and useful, not only to the reader, but also to the entire organization. And it is considerably more likely to attract the attention—and attendance—of people who have not attended regularly in the past. The problem here, of course, is that the planning has to be done far in advance for an organization to provide that kind of information to the readers of the newsletter where that information is publicized. How far in advance? Ideally, a year, but in the short term, at least six weeks.

Here is how it works. The deadlines for most parish newsletters (at least those published monthly) usually fall somewhere just past the middle of the month. If a group wants complete information about the program for its regular monthly meeting included in the congregation's newsletter, and it is meeting in the last week of the next month, it has to have every detail of planning for that meeting in place before the newsletter's deadline. This could take a minimum of six weeks.

Without that kind of advance planning, however, the organization is perceived as the same group of people meeting at the same time and place once every month to do the same thing that they have always done. "Same old, same old" does not attract nor hold new members.

When the newsletter editor, wanting to write and publish the most complete story possible, calls for more information about an event earlier than the planning has been completed, it can create some substantial tensions. The same is true of all other aspects of a congregation's life and work where publicity is wanted but complete information is hard to come by before a publication deadline.

Specific plans for stewardship and evangelism emphases calls for frequent articles that highlight them often and well in advance. Members are eager to read reports of progress on particular programs—or the lack of progress—on a regular basis. If a construction program is being considered to enlarge and improve a congregation's facilities, good planning committees begin informing the congregation as soon as an initial design has been drawn, especially if construction concepts were suggested by members of the congregation in earlier meetings. Once reports begin, members want to be kept up to date on progress until the building is completed.

Newsletter articles might include an invitation for members to respond to the publication of a simple floor plan soon after it is available. Architects and building committee members, creative and thorough as they are, have been known to miss supposedly simple things like doors opening the wrong way for the best access and inadequate storage space in the areas where it is needed most.

Editors most often want to point to the future, but sometimes, they dare not forget to report significant actions that have happened in the recent past. Such reports might include actions of the council or standing committees (in the form of news stories, not minutes), reports on particularly interesting and useful programs sponsored by the congregation's organizations, and evaluation of programs that were changed or have recently begun.

Those meetings and programs are important, but it is not as important to the story to report who served the tea, cake, and Jell-O at those meetings, or what games were played in connection with a special program, or who conducted the opening devotions at the board meeting. (See chapter 6 for content ideas and organization, and chapter 8 for the editor's responsibility and authority.)

To Educate

So what topics do you include to fit and fill the purpose of education in your parish publications? Start by asking and answering several sets of questions. The first set deals with congregational stewardship and personal benevolence.

Connecting to Larger Concerns

How many members of your congregation are informed about the various local, regional, national, and international programs of charitable giving and the organizations they help to support with the offerings they give during worship services? (Many religious organizations incorporate all of that charitable activity in the term *benevolence*.)

Can they name and locate the colleges and seminaries supported by the faith group of which they are members?

Do they know where international mission activity is sponsored and the kinds of mission work that go on in those places around the world?

Can they connect current events in those places with the ministries they are supporting there?

Are they familiar with the ecumenical interactions of social-service agencies financed by the national organization, how much they cost, and how effective those interactions are?

Would they give more to support missionaries in the far corners of the world as well as the United States if they knew about how and to whom they minister and had some gauges that demonstrated the difficulty of that commissioned work? Probably. People give to causes about which they are informed.

Would they respond more quickly with more dollars if they knew about your faith group's presence in countries and regions devastated by famine, flood, drought, epidemic, and earthquake? Most likely.

Would they be more alert to community concerns if they knew what kinds of things the religious organization at large and their own congregation were trying to do in ministries to abused spouses and children, homeless men, women, and children, and people with addictions who live in their neighborhood? Without a doubt.

How many members of your congregation know which schools (high school, colleges, seminaries) are supported by their faith group, where they are located, tuition costs and financial aid, and something about their faculty and curricular strengths? The more they know about these educational opportunities, the stronger those institutions and your congregation will be and the more likely it is that young members of your congregation will find their way into those high-quality schools. Do they also know about scholarship programs sponsored by your congregation for its members?

Educational information on such matters is quickly available on the Web sites of most faith organizations. It can be copied, edited, and made to fit in your parish newsletters and service folders with a minimum of effort. If your congregation does not yet have Internet access, the same information is available by mail.

In many religious organizations, mailings filled with such information are sent to the pastor's office on a regular basis. If not, it can be ordered by telephone from the nearest judicatory office and received by regular mail within a few days. (The advantage of Web sites is that the information does not have to be keyboarded again to be included in the parish publication. It can simply be copied and pasted into the parish publication.)

If they are not already doing so, pastors can be encouraged to pass on information they receive on worldwide ministry to a member or committee of the congregation. Then those people can recommend programs the congregation might support through its annual benevolence budget. They can also help determine which educational material might be included regularly in parish communications.

Learning about Practices and Traditions

A second set of questions regarding the educational purpose of parish communication deals with practices and traditions that might be something of a mystery to some members. I'm talking here about functions and operations, not faith.

For instance, if your congregation uses a liturgical form of worship, how many of the worshipers are conversant with the various forms and parts of the liturgy, why they are used, and what they mean?

Increasing numbers of congregations are using more than one worship book during a service. How many worshipers—members and visitors—can identify which worship book is which and when to make the shifts from one to the other during the service?

How many members remember from their catechetical or Sunday school instruction the historical background of their creeds and the evolutionary nature of the translation of the traditional prayers now being prayed in your worship services?

If your congregation uses paraments on the chancel furniture and changes the color with the liturgical seasons, what does that mean for the people in the pew? Would it enhance their worship experience to be reminded periodically of what those colors and symbols stand for?

A series of brief paragraphs, used regularly in both the worship service guide and the periodic newsletter, can help to fill these gaps.

Becoming More Comfortable with Worship

A third set of questions deals with the content of worship. How many members and visitors to services at your place of worship know why certain texts are read and how they are chosen? Liturgical congregations can introduce their members to the word *pericope* and explain its significance. (*Pericope*—sometimes called *lectionary*—is a list of appointed scripture readings and psalms for all of the worship days of a year in a religious organization.)

Assuming that the sermon preached during each worship service is based on one of those pericope texts, think about announcing the texts, themes, and outlines of those sermons in the parish newsletter one month in advance. Then repeat each sermon outline (probably revised by this time) in the worship service folder so that people will have a powerful aid to following and understanding the words and ideas that flow from the preacher. Both the people and the pastor will enjoy a more significant worship experience.

Whether your congregation uses those same pericope texts or ones chosen by other criteria, an alternative feature in the parish newsletter would give textual references and ask several questions about each regarding their content and meaning (both historical and contemporary). The feature could be an invitation to come to the weekly Bible study for adults throughout the coming month. Make sure brief answers to the questions can be found in the next issue near the new set of Bible studies for that month. That practice alone will help to build readership.

Introducing the Congregation to Itself

A fourth set of suggestions helps the congregation to become better acquainted with itself. Introduce the people of the congregation to each other. Even if your congregation's membership is comparatively small, many of the people do not know each other as well as they would like to.

Start with the members of the council, the parish education teachers, or the support staff (secretaries and custodians). When new members are received, those families are natural subjects for stories to help them get acquainted.

Every one of these personality features is potentially the story of a family, not just an individual. Even if the subject of the story is a single person, she has some family somewhere. And in nearly every instance, that person will want to talk about parents and siblings. Features on families talk about what work the spouses do, who their children are, and their likes and dislikes. If they just moved into the community, what was responsible for the relocation? If they have lived there a long time, why have they stayed around so long? What do they like about the congregation, and what do they hope might be changed?

If you have the capability to print photos with good quality in your parish publications (see chapter 10), make sure a picture of the whole family in the feature is included. If capabilities in photo reproduction are limited (they still are in most congregations), then post a photo of the family on a convenient bulletin board together with the story from your newsletter. Point out the location of the bulletin board occasionally in both the newsletter and worship service guide, and encourage everyone to check it regularly.

To Motivate

Motivation is difficult work. Yet, if parish publications—particularly the newsletter—are to do their basic job, they must be motivators. Otherwise, all of the time, effort, and money that goes into their production is largely wasted.

But what triggers motivation? Motivation happens when people have been informed and educated. That is when they can see either personal or congregational significance in their own and their family's involvement in the meeting, program, emphasis, or worship service.

If members of the congregation do not have adequate information (Who? What? When? Where? Why/How?) that reports creative and potentially interesting programs, they will not be motivated to be involved. If they are not educated regarding their place as one part of their faith group at large and the ministries that faith group makes possible, they will have no cosmic sense of the meaningfulness of their involvement.

Consider the nonmember who recently has became a prospect for membership (I am talking about evangelism here). That person begins to receive your congregation's newsletter but finds little in it except incomplete information and little education regarding how the congregation sees itself in its faith group as well as in the world. How likely is it that such a person will be eager to join hands with you in membership?

Some congregations try to overcome their information and education gaps with a panoply of supposedly motivational clichés. They pepper every article with at least one. But admonitions such as: "Mark your calendar"; "Don't miss this meeting"; "Plan now to attend"; "Y'all Come"; or the slightly more subtle "Why not come?" (negative questions lead to negative answers) are no substitute for substantive facts. Such clichés have a carping sound. They do not motivate. In some cases they might even repulse.

Too often, newsletters and worship service folder announcements are written as if everyone who reads them is already motivated to respond positively to every opportunity to get together with other members no matter what is on the agenda. That might work for the most loyal and the least perceptive. It does not work for either the already too-busy members or the marginal members who long ago fell away from regular participation in the work and support of both the local congregation and the wider faith community.

They need more. They need complete information and continual education if they are to come back to active membership or make the calendar-related sacrifices necessary to be as active as both they and their congregation would like them to be. They also need congregation-wide sensitivity so that opportunities for participation are as free from complications as possible.

15

How long has it been since all the leaders of your congregation have studied your organization's demographics? Do women's groups still meet exclusively in the afternoon? If so, they have systematically cut out participation by women who are employed outside the home. And how can stay-at-home dads participate in afternoon meetings? What is offered for childcare services at the same time meetings take place? Single parents need help with taking care of their children. Two-parent families do as well. Baby-sitters are not only expensive, they are hard to get during weeknights. If childcare is not provided, most single parents cannot come. If childcare is provided, it could make possible one more opportunity for some significant congregation-related, Bible-based education. Groups that expect to attract parents to their meetings do everything possible to make it easier for them to attend.

To Edify

Writing to edify—"to build up or increase the faith," according to Webster's Dictionary—is extremely difficult. Once in a while, a person can write a piece, push back from the keyboard, read the screen, and say, "That's almost edifying." But the times that happens are few—particularly in parish newsletters.

But pastors keep on trying. Month after month they turn out less than satisfying essays to add what they hope is an inspiring message to the periodic newsletter. They talk about summer vacations, a seasonal insight triggered most often by the weather, occasionally a disguised conversation from a counseling session, once in awhile an unfinished insight into a particular verse of scripture. On rare occasions, some readers might get warm, fuzzy feelings as they work their way through this little essay. More often, they wonder why they took the time to read this piece and, even worse, why someone took the time to write it.

Adding to the problem, far too many pastors insist that this piece of marginal prose fills the front page of the newsletter. Why? Here is one of those places where the "because we've always done it this way" answer is the primary response. That's a little worse than no response at all.

Furthermore, many pastors have told me in workshops and seminars I've conducted that they have never liked the assignment, and are often at a loss to know what to write. According to the secretaries or newsletter editors who must include this material, the pastors more often than not have a hard time finishing and delivering their efforts before the deadline. Let's try to dissect the problem.

First, the subject matter. Parishioners have the chance for edification by words from the pastor during the sermon of every worship service. That nearly keeps the pastor busy all by itself. Attempting one more shot at inspiration in a "pocket sermon" on the front page of the monthly newsletter runs the risk of being redundant at best and dangerously peripheral at worst.

If the pastor feels that he has to have a personal imprimatur on the contents of every newsletter from his parish, that publication, or at least the person who has the responsibility to put it together, is in trouble (see chapter 8). If the pastor insists that his attempt at edification has to be in the prime space for the congregation's newsletter, the publication and its editor are in even bigger trouble. At best, that kind of content is most closely related to an editorial in any public newspaper. Where are editorials printed in a newspaper? With rare exception, newspaper editorials are always printed on the inside pages of the paper's first section, maybe as far back as page 10, 14, or even 20.

The front cover is the prime location of any publication. Therefore, in a parish newsletter, it is always reserved and used for the prime news story in the congregation at that time. For example:

- The series of Lenten services will begin in the middle of the next month. That's the story—with sermon texts, themes, service dates and times, and special activities like a soup and bread supper before every service.
- A totally new program of cross-generational scripture study is going to be introduced next month. That is the big news for the front page.
- The stewardship committee is calling for a 10 percent increase in giving by every member of the congregation next year. That is news for the front page.
- The council has just voted to spend $250,000 on the improvement of the congregation's parking lot. That is the front-page story.
- The council has approved the parish education committee's recommendation to make a major shift in the curriculum materials

that will be used next fall for the congregation's education program. That would need front-page coverage.

Now the pastor's letter can come into clearer focus. It can use subjective language to talk about the objective reporting in that front-page story. The pastor's letter now becomes a relevant and persuasive editorial that supports the facts and encourages the people to be active participants in the program. The tie between news or events or official action is one more thing that also takes planning and coordination.

The Question of Relevance

A final question needs to be considered. Is the content of the newsletter and other parish communications relevant to the work of the congregation? And is that same content relevant to the lives of the members and nonmembers of the congregation who receive it?

Stephen Wilbers, a Minneapolis consultant who offers training seminars in effective business writing, writes an "Effective Writing" column for the business section of the *Star Tribune* in Minneapolis. His column on April 12, 2002, included the following:

> If I were asked to judge the effectiveness of a random sample of newsletters, I would begin by sorting them into four categories: slick and interesting; slick but irrelevant; amateurish but interesting; and amateurish and irrelevant.
>
> My criteria would be appearance, relevance to the intended audience and quality of writing.
>
> The initial determination between slick and amateurish, based primarily on appearance, would be simple: Do the graphics, layout, visual variety, etc., make the publication visually appealing?
>
> The next step, assessing relevance to the intended audience, also would be easy.
>
> I would begin not by reading the text, but by skimming the headlines to see what proportion of the articles promoted the organization (material related to reputation, history, internal matters, etc.), and what proportion appealed directly to the readers' interests and concerns (advice, information, resources, etc.).
>
> In other words, I would ask, does the newsletter focus on itself

or on the reader? To the creators of the inward-looking or self-absorbed publications, I would say, take a lesson from good conversationalists: It's not about you. It's about what is interesting or useful to your audience. . . .

While your congregation's periodic newsletter revolves around the four purposes of information, education, motivation, and edification, the relevance of its content for the people who read it undergirds its effectiveness for your congregation.

- Information is objective language reporting on what will be happening.
- Education, also objective, hooks the member of her local congregation to the national and international faith community and to daily discipleship.
- Motivation happens when members get excited about the worship, study, and ministries their congregation offers, and they know they will miss something important in their day-to-day lives if they choose not to participate.
- Edification is a coveted by-product of information, education, and motivation. Unfortunately, it probably won't happen often in your newsletter. But on those rare occasions when it does happen, say a little prayer of thanksgiving.

All four purposes must be handled in such a way that they are unmistakably relevant to the life and faith of all the intended readers of a publication. When all four purposes come together with that kind of relevance, they can add up to an enhanced awareness of evangelism and stewardship in every member of the congregation. And is that not the mission and ministry to which your congregation and its people have been called?

The stewardship, evangelism, and education implications of good communication are an integral part of *Getting the Word Out* and are made more obvious in later chapters. That's what the ministry of communication is all about. But all your purposes will be for naught if you have not adequately analyzed your audiences.

When analyzed, every congregation's audience is plural, not singular. It includes old and young, women and men, active and inactive, prospects and media, and more. The changing proportions of those kinds of groupings and the relationships of one audience to another need to be analyzed regularly. And when they are, that analysis helps to determine not only the kinds of ministries and services a congregation provides, but also the nature of the publications and public relations program that a congregation creates and puts in play to promote them.

That's the heart of the next chapter.

3

Who Is Your Audience?

Who is the audience for all the publications or other means of communication that emanate from your congregation? In other words, who is expected to read them? That's an easy question, right? The automatic answer: all the people of the congregation. Unfortunately, the question is not that easy, and that answer is not adequate. It needs a lot more thought and a much more complete analysis.

Every congregation is made up of varieties of people. The people responsible for the congregation's communication program must know who those varieties are, how they are divided, and how they are identified. Let's examine a relatively normal model—a midsize congregation of 750 confirmed members in a town of 20,000. The audiences are best illustrated with a series of concentric circles.

Starting at the Core

The circles start at the center with the "core." These people, always a relatively small group, can be depended upon to attend every regular worship service—and the special seasonal services as well. They probably have been members of the congregation longer than anyone else. They will volunteer for tasks whether or not they have the talents and the abilities to do the work in the way it needs to be done.

They are the "pillars of the congregation," and God bless them. They are needed, and they are appreciated. But sometimes they are the people to whom we listen too much. They can be depended upon after every worship service to compliment the pastor at the door on his sermon. And sometimes the pastor knows the sermon was not that good. The pastor knows the exegesis was weak, the outline barely hung together, and the content drew on far too many warmed-over clichés.

But, if you are the pastor, you appreciate the compliment. It gives you a little emotional fuel to begin the next week.

Our problems with the core are compounded when these same faithful people tell us they think the newsletter is really great when in actuality we know it needs substantial improvement. Estimated number or core people in a congregation of 750 confirmed members: 25 people or 3.3 percent.

Keeping Track of the Muscle

The next circle is made up of the people in the congregation who might be called the "muscle."

These are the people who are the congregation's central leadership base. They are busy people, with their families, jobs, and community service. Even though their time is limited, their motivation to service in the congregation also causes them to be busy with their faith group. They are members of the council. They teach in the congregation's education program. They sing in the choir. They read the lessons during worship services, and those with strong singing voices serve as cantors. They make creative and far-reaching suggestions for improvement and expansion of the congregation's ministry.

In more fortunate congregations, some of those in the "muscle circle" are graduates of church-related colleges and universities or are taking courses in continuing education. Whether or not they are college educated (and many who make up the muscle of congregations are not), they are among the congregation's leaders in their personal stewardship. They give proportionately of their income, not only to their faith group, but also to other organizations in the community and beyond where funds are needed. They are sensitive to the needs of those who are less fortunate and try to help in whatever ways they can.

People who are the muscle of a congregation can be expected to be present for worship at least three out of every four services each month. Most importantly, while they affirm the ministry of which they are a part, they also will give constructive criticism of programs and preaching and whatever else might need a forceful voice when necessary. The group that makes up the muscle is indispensable to the ministry and mission of the congregation. Estimated number in a congregation of 750: 225 people or 30 percent. So far, that accounts for just a bit more than 30 percent of the congregation.

Figure 3-1
Audience Analysis Circles

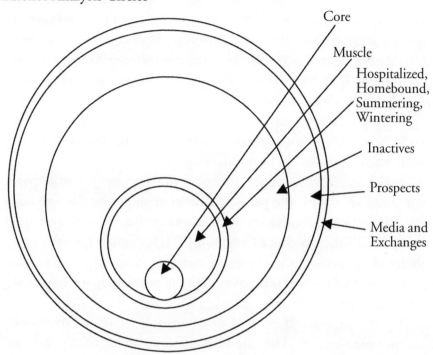

Core

Muscle

Hospitalized,
Homebound,
Summering,
Wintering

Inactives

Prospects

Media and
Exchanges

Dealing with Inactives

A third circle calls for our attention, and perhaps it needs the most attention of all. The third circle includes "inactive" members. These are the people who are on the list of members, but they are almost strangers to the congregation and its mission. They can usually be seen in the sanctuary during the major religious festivals and holy days. Some of them might come to worship once every couple of months or so. They are there for the benchmarks of life: marriage, baptism, confirmation, funerals.

At some point in the lives of currently inactive members, membership in the congregation was important. But some place along the line, dissatisfaction and disillusionment set in. Or maybe it was just apathy and inertia. The congregation no longer seemed relevant as other interests got in the way of corporate faith and worship. Participation in worship services became less and less frequent until attendance dropped off completely.

Some people who join a faith group through adult membership orientation are excited about this new foundation in their lives when they become members. But commitment to the faith turns out to be a distant rather than a personal concept, or something happens in the congregation that "turns them off," and they slowly and silently slip away from any idea of active service.

Inactives are a major constituency of every congregation. In the model of a 750-member church, nearly 450 confirmed members—about 60 percent—might be in this category.

In one sense, the inactives are the parish newsletter's most important audience. Often, the periodic newsletter might be the one and only connection that awakens a link between their present lives and their past affiliation with the faith group. But for that to have any possibility of happening, the newsletter must be designed to invite the inactives to read content that has a chance of motivating them back to active participation.

Too many congregations have given up on bringing inactives back to active membership. They are tolerated for awhile. Then someone decides they are more of a problem than they are worth. (After all, congregational payments to their regional judicatories are sometimes based at least partly on the number of members on the rosters, and it takes money to produce and mail those "extra" copies of congregational mailings.) So they are purged from the list of members. The evangelism committee clears its conscience and stops wondering what to do about them. And the newsletter, perhaps the only contact that has kept them in touch with the ministries of their congregation, no longer arrives in their mailbox to compete for their attention.

Keeping the "In-between" Circle in Mind

Someplace in between the circles representing the muscle and the inactives is a separate, thinner circle. Perhaps it is intertwined at the edges. It includes persons who are homebound, hospitalized, or under 24-hour care. It also includes those who have moved from the community for most of a season because they either have gone south in the winter as "snowbirds" or gone north in the summer as lakeside cabin dwellers.

Depending on the season, this intertwined group might include anywhere from 5 to 25 percent of the congregation.

It is easy for the "home congregations" to lose touch with these people. They won't get the worship service folders because they are not attending worship in the congregation where they are members. They won't get the periodic newsletter because the post office does not forward third-class mail. They might, however, be attending institutional chapel services or visiting congregations near their winter or summer homes. All of that can create an interesting member exchange as congregations in the communities where the people go to "get away" might see them attending worship and participating in special programs. Those congregations might want to factor such short-term attendees into their audience analysis. They might even want to do some special scheduling and advertising to attract and serve them.

Congregations can put procedures in place by which worship service folders could be delivered personally to those who are homebound or under around-the-clock care by lay members of the congregation, preferably on the day the worship service was held. Perhaps these "deliverers" are members of an evangelism subcommittee. Maybe they are simply a visitation task force. At any rate, they can provide a much-appreciated service.

It is important that a congregation's mailing list is checked regularly to make sure short-term changes of address are reflected whenever the status of any of these people changes or they make a periodic move. Young people away at college or in the armed services need the same kind of attention so they receive the newsletter regularly at their new places of residence.

Being Alert for Prospects

The next circle varies greatly in size. It includes all the "prospects," people in the community who are looking for a faith home and have visited your congregation. The population of this circle varies greatly from congregation to congregation.

If your congregation is located in a newly established suburban area, the list of prospects will be large and will probably grow every week. Its growth is fed with the names and addresses written by worship service visitors in guest books, on pew cards, or on know-your-neighbor forms passed up and down the pews to be filled out during the service.

Leaders of small two- or three-point parishes in rural areas across the country sometimes think their congregations have little opportunity for any kind of prospect list at all. That's an unfortunate mistake. It is true that the populations of agricultural areas are in decline, and few, if any, new people are moving in to take the places of those who are moving out.

But many people in the populations that remain have never been connected with any faith group, have let earlier connections disintegrate, or intentionally have broken those connections because they decided the congregation was not really interested in their problems and was not meeting their needs. Some of them think they have never been asked to be part of the life and mission of your congregation. Some of them are so concerned with survival from month to month and year to year that they have convinced themselves they do not have time for anything other than working the land or running their small, supporting agribusinesses.

Congregations surrounded by such hurting people might try to remind them in gentle and substantive ways that they originally were established to help the people in the community and they still consider such support a vital part of their mission. Some of them can be influenced to see the congregation as an ally, a friend that offers an alternative to despair, and a foundation of faith offering help and hope, love and life.

Some congregations have printed door hangers and had their young people hang them on every residence in the town and country in a circle extending ten miles around them. The hangers invited people to participate in worship and other programs. And some of them responded by becoming active members of the congregation.

Other faith groups looked at the problems—psychological, physical, and financial—that plagued their agricultural community and planned and publicized a series of workshops and seminars where residents could find some help and hope. And many of those people moved from the category of prospect to the status of member.

Most important, the list of prospects (large or small) is a major part of the mailing list for the periodic newsletter and every other piece of printed communication produced by a congregation.

Tapping into the Help of Media and Exchanges

The final circle includes two groups: "media" and "exchanges." Most congregations spend far too little time and energy courting the media. At the same time, they complain about media coverage of faith group activity—either the media are not interested enough, or the interest they show is ill informed, inaccurate, or out of context.

Media Are People, Too

The first thing to keep in mind when dealing with the media is recognizing that the media are people—one person at a time. Pastors and other leaders in a congregation want to know the person who is responsible for religious news in the local paper, radio station, and TV station. And those media personnel need and want to know the pastor and other congregational leaders.

It happens like this. First, either the pastor or a layperson designated as the congregation's media representative calls the newspaper and radio and TV stations and finds out who usually handles religious news.

Then appointments are set up for meetings with each of those media contacts. Perhaps the meetings can be scheduled in the local coffee shop, but if at all possible they are always away from either one's desk. The conversations revolve around the congregation: How many members? How many usually worship? What special programs are offered, and whom do they serve?

The media are invited to attend worship services to get a better feel for the congregation, its program, and its people. It is also important to learn specific media deadlines, and the optimum times for a news story to appear on a media person's desk or in their e-mail in order for it to get adequate consideration for inclusion in the next paper or broadcast.

Media personnel are also alerted to the openness of the pastor to being "on call" as someone who could comment occasionally on theological and social implications of breaking news stories and community concerns. The pastor also offers to work with the local ministerium to set up a schedule in which every interested pastor in the community could write a regular column, or tape a brief radio or TV message on a rotating basis.

The representative also shows all the media people the most recent copy of the congregation's monthly newsletter and offers to add their names to the mailing list. Acknowledging that media people receive more material than they have time to read, the congregation's representative suggests that a quick glance at their parish newsletter might reveal a special program in the congregation or something out of the ordinary being done by one of the members that deserves wider circulation.

After all, the congregational representative says, media people have developed a "nose for news" that the pastor and leaders of her congregation probably do not have. Consequently, some really good stories might go unreported. The following personal example illustrates how this works.

I started my ministry as pastor of a mission congregation of the former American Lutheran Church in Painesville, Ohio. The congregation was growing and a small, attractive unit of the church had been built. Serving a mission congregation, I was covetous of every bit of publicity the church could get and I made it a point to meet the religion editor of the small daily paper serving the community within the first week I was there. We understood each other's needs and developed a good working relationship.

Early in December I was thinking about what could be done of a special nature for the congregation's first New Year's Eve service. The new church had been built without a bell, so we did not have that sound and symbol to lean on as something unique to the worship service.

It was the first year of the merger that had formed the American Lutheran Church. In celebration, the time had been designated "Year of Jubilee," and a small plastic ram's horn had been sent to every pastor in the synod. It was a bit on the ugly side. I tried to blow it, but I was unable to get a sound out of that gray plastic replica, so set it in its little wooden stand near the top of my office bookcase and promptly forgot about it.

I was not making much progress on the New Year's Eve service, until a teenage member of the congregation stopped in one afternoon. He was a trumpeter. As we chatted, I remembered that ram's horn, showed it to him, and asked if he could blow it. That teenager put that ugly little horn to his lips and blew the most awful, ungodly wail I had heard in a long time. It was beautiful.

We had our New Year's Eve service. That teenage trumpet player would blow out the old year and blow in the new with that ram's horn. It was biblical; it had great symbolism; it was fun.

I wrote a three-paragraph news story and took it to my friend, the religion editor of the newspaper. Now luck sometimes plays a hand in events, even in faith groups. As it happened, when I took my story to the religion editor, she was just wondering what she was going to do with her New Year's Eve page that might make it something special.

When that story hit the press, it had been expanded to take up the top one-fourth of the newspaper page and included a two-column photograph of the teenager blowing the ram's horn. It was the kind of positive publicity that a mission congregation would not have been able to buy in ages. And it was possible largely because of a strong working relationship between a pastor and a reporter.

Media are one of the essential audiences for a congregation's periodic newsletter. For more information on media relations, see chapter 9.

The Value of Exchanges

Exchanges are nearly as important as the media piece of that circle. Make a list of congregations—some nearby, some far away, some similar in size and ministry, some totally different—and ask if they will put your congregation's name on their mailing list in exchange for regular mailings of your congregation's promotional materials. Some of the pastor's seminary friends as well as some of the pastor's and the editor's college friends can be tapped as potential resources. And then change that list at least once a year.

The result of such an exchange practice will be a panoply of ideas for programs and ways to promote them that you or members of your congregation might not have thought about on your own. The ideas will fall into several categories: new ways to approach stewardship, evangelism, and parish education; approaches to content that will broaden the readability of your own newsletter; and technological advances that you have the capability for but had not yet put into use.

The writer of Ecclesiastes had some advice appropriate to the borrowing of ideas from your exchange list:

What has been is what will be, and what has been done is what will be done; there is nothing new under the sun. Is there a thing of which it is said, "See, this is new"? It has already been, in the ages before us. The people of long ago are not remembered, nor will there be any remembrance of people yet to come by those who come after them. (Ecclesiastes 1:9-11)

Figuring the Percentages

Now look at those circles of audience in a different way. Starting at the center, the "core" and the "muscle" make up the bulk of the people who attend worship in your congregation on any given Sunday. According to national statistics from several polls, only 30 to 35 percent of an average congregation's membership can be expected to attend weekly worship services regularly.

Those are the people—usually the only people—who receive and have a chance to read the worship service guide, otherwise known as the bulletin. Yet some congregations seem to put all their publicity and promotion eggs in that one small basket. If that is happening in your congregation, that leaves 65 to 70 percent of the people without a clue regarding the organization's schedule, ongoing ministry, and special programs.

The periodic newsletter, on the other hand, has the possibility of reaching 100 percent of the congregation, its prospects, and the media at least once a month. The newsletter is the vehicle that includes a detailed monthly calendar, the agenda for the monthly council meetings as well as the annual meeting, and monthly updates on attendance and accumulative giving and whether it is ahead or behind budget projections. It also provides detailed notices of the regular meetings of women, youth, men, singles, couples, seniors, and every other special group and what is planned for all those future programs.

The newsletter might even include notes on the texts and sermon themes for the coming weeks, personality features on council members, Sunday school teachers, and other leaders, and educational paragraphs regarding the ministries of the state and national organizations to which the congregation belongs and gives financial support. (See chapter 6 for a broader range of ideas.)

Given that kind of publicity in the newsletter, the bulletin (in addition to being the guide to the worship service) only has to provide brief reminders of the things that all the members have already had the opportunity to read about and mark on their calendar.

Setting Up Your Own Demographic Survey

That's the way a good publications program works. But how can a congregation make this happen? Start with an in-house demographic survey. Ask an existing group—it could be the young people, the ushers, a special task force—to analyze the congregation's membership. You might want to use the "Self-Study and Analysis Form" in appendix A.

First, you need statistics—numbers that can be used to analyze the nature and makeup of the audiences in your congregation. Count the people in each of the congregation's audiences; then calculate the percentage for each audience as described in the circles and listed in appendix A.

Now break down the membership in terms of men, women, youth, married, single, divorced, and any other category that might be useful in planning the ministries offered (or to be offered) by your congregation. Perhaps the self-study and analysis team will need to conduct a special survey to learn some of the information it wants.

It also might be important to know how many families have situations where both spouses work outside the home. Perhaps it would be useful to know how many families need to use childcare for at least part of every weekday. Your congregation might want to pay special attention to some of these kinds of concerns when it schedules worship services and programs. If that happens, the congregation's publications program would want to announce the new programs so the entire congregation is aware of the new approaches to ministry. It might even be important to devise special means of communication (perhaps e-mail and the Web; see chapter 11) as better ways to keep these busy families informed.

New ministries sometimes drive special communications programs, and sometimes communications concerns drive planning for special programs. It can work both ways. See chapters 6 and 7 for content ideas that will help to serve all of your congregation's audiences with information and education they can use and will act upon.

Now you have a well-defined picture of your congregation. Once you have the numbers, you also have a better foundation to decide which kinds of publications can serve your congregation best and the mission and purpose statements that define what those publications and public relations programs should be. Keep these statements brief and succinct. Draw upon information in the chapters of this book designated on the form. That material will help clarify what you want the various publications in your communications arsenal to do to enhance your congregation's total ministry.

Now it's time to get more specific.

4

Making Your Words Readable

All examples cited are actual notices and articles found in worship service guides and newsletters within recent decades. Names and places have been changed. Typefaces and line lengths are similar to those in the original items. The rewrites often include material added out of the author's imagination in order to provide enough information to complete the story as it should have been written in the first place.

The following item was printed years ago from a worship service folder for a small congregation in Iowa.

```
The new envelopes for our debt retirement fund are
being handed out this morning. Many of our members
have some envelopes left from last year and could
use them instead of getting a new pack, but some of
our members use these envelopes each Sunday and
have run out of envelopes in their old packs. It
was decided to give each one a new pack whether
there are some left in their old packs or not and
that each one should have the same number as his or
her number on the other envelopes. So will each one
take a new pack with your new number and throw
whatever old envelopes you have left away.
```

If ever there was a case of too much information, this is it. That single announcement took nearly one-third of the space on one page of a four-page 8½ x 5½ inch bulletin. Perhaps the foreboding frugality of the members, who could not abide throwing anything away, forced such a labored explanation. Perhaps absolutely nothing else was happening in this congregation and the bulletin writer was desperate to write anything to fill up all that extra space. More likely, ideas of the economy of language and questions of readability were never considered.

In any event, that announcement can be edited to a few lines:

```
New debt retirement fund envelopes are here. Please
pick yours up from the table in the narthex, throw
away any of your old envelopes, and begin using the
new ones with your next gift.
```

Dealing with the Five Ws

Where do you start when you use written language for parish publications? You start at the beginning. Start with the facts. Journalists begin with answers to five questions: Who? What? When? Where? Why or How?

If you are asked to be responsible for written communication in your congregation, you have just been assigned to be a journalist—even though your assignment is expected to be on a more modest level than assignments handled by professional newspaper reporters and editors. Consider the writing of an announcement for your parish newsletter as an assignment in journalism. Here are the facts you are given for the story:

- The women's organization in the congregation will be meeting.
- The group is an auxiliary of Immanuel Lutheran Church in Prairie, Minnesota.
- It is their regular meeting, and it will be held as usual in the congregation's fellowship hall.
- The date of the meeting is Thursday, March 28, 2003.
- The meeting will begin at 2 P.M.

Analyze it this way around the five Ws.

- Who? Immanuel Lutheran Women of the Church.
- What? Regular monthly meeting.
- When? 2 P.M., March 28, 2003.
- Where? Immanuel Lutheran Church Fellowship Hall.
- Why or How? Not known, unless you want to say the group has always met on the third Thursday of the month.

Now comes the task of writing the newsletter article. First, give a priority ranking to the information in the five Ws. What's most and least important?

Since it is a regular meeting, the time and place (when and where) are not the most significant. Consequently, announcements and news stories should never start with, "On March 28, at 2 P.M. . . ." The date and time of an organization's regular meeting is not the most important information in that report. The why or how is not answered by the available information, so that is not a factor. That leaves the who and what as most important. Now the newsletter story practically writes itself.

```
Immanuel Lutheran Women will hold their regu-
lar meeting at the church in Fellowship Hall
at 2:00 p.m. on Thursday, March 28.
```

That's not much of an item, is it? It is essentially an announcement to remind members of what most of them already know. The absence of information regarding the program makes this meeting particularly mundane at best and not very inviting to anyone who is not already an active member of the group. Remember those inactive members?

So what is an editor to do? If you are in that position, you have two choices: (1) print what you have or (2) go back to the person who was the source of the original material and suggest that the organization would have a much bigger and more active membership and attendance if it would provide more substantive information about programs, causes, and personnel involved in the organization.

After that conversation, the facts might have been fleshed out. Now they include:

Who?   Barbara Olson, medical missionary to Tanzania, Africa, currently home on furlough, born and raised on a farm near Prairie.
Penny Quince, a member of Women of the Church.
Sally Messner, president of the women's group.

What?   An illustrated program entitled "Medical Emergency in Africa," in which Olson will report on her past 10 years of experience as a nurse in several clinics spread throughout the country.
Quince: will conduct the Bible study on the apostle Paul's letter to the Ephesians.

The when and where? The same as the first set of facts.

The why or how? Take on educational and emotional perspective.

Rewritten with the additional information, the story might look something like this:

> Barbara Olson, medical missionary to Tanzania, will present "Medical Emergency in Africa," an illustrated program, during the regular meeting of the Immanuel Lutheran Women of the Church in Fellowship Hall at 2:00 p.m. on Thursday, March 21.
>
> Olson is currently home on furlough after spending the past ten years as a nurse in several clinics in Tanzania. Born and raised on a farm near Prairie, she is known personally by many of the people who are members of Immanuel.
>
> Tanzania is one of the 45 countries served by programs of the Division for Global Mission of the Evangelical Lutheran Church in America (ELCA) of which Immanuel is a member congregation.
>
> The usual monthly Bible study will focus on the Apostle Paul's letter to the Ephesians, and will be led by Penny Quince, a long-time member of the Women of the Church.
>
> The business meeting will include action on a possible major gift to the Tanzania mission field out of the Women of the Church treasury, according to President Sally Messner. She said, "The presentation by Missionary Olson will make this a particularly exciting meeting, and all of the women of Immanuel are urged to attend whether or not they are members."

Note how the story is developed. The facts are covered in the order of their priority as significant information that will attract the attention, and maybe the attendance, of not only the regular, active members, but also other members of the congregation who might be interested in the program. In fact, the program for this meeting might be so interesting that the spouses of members could be invited to attend as guests.

If the group really were interested in attracting larger attendance, it would probably change its meeting time to 7 P.M. rather than 2 P.M.

Most women employed outside the home simply cannot attend an afternoon meeting no matter how much they would like to, and many women today are employed outside the home.

Turning Over the Pyramid

Also note the style of writing, which uses a journalistic technique known as "inverted pyramid." It works like this.

Figure 4-1
Inverted Pyramid

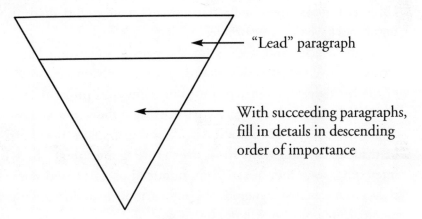

"Lead" paragraph

With succeeding paragraphs, fill in details in descending order of importance

The first paragraph—one or two sentences known as the "lead"—provides brief and basic answers to all of the five Ws and is about 20 words in length.

About 50 years ago, students in beginning journalism classes were taught that all of the five Ws had to be included in the first sentence, and the first sentence could not be longer than 35 words. A generation later the rules were changed. Then, all the Ws still had to be answered in the first sentence, but that first sentence should not be longer than 18 words. Today, a good journalist still includes answers to all five Ws in the first 18 to 25 words, but those words might form two sentences and maybe even two paragraphs. Today's pattern for the lead provides the most interesting reading.

After the lead paragraph or paragraphs, every subsequent paragraph amplifies and explains information already written, but the information is in a descending order of importance and less and less necessary to completing the facts of the story. It is interesting material and amplifies the facts for those who take the time to read it, but it is not essential information. Journalistic writing is vastly different from an essay where the writer starts out with a stated hypothesis and concludes with the answer. The journalistic writer starts by announcing the conclusive answer and then names and identifies the resources and the details of the argument that brought the person or persons to that conclusion. That is why writing in the style of the inverted pyramid is the keystone of journalistic reporting.

Writing in inverted pyramids has another use. Newsletter and bulletin editors frequently run into the problem of "too much material, too little space." That problem is not unique to parish publications. Large city newspapers, national newsmagazines, and institutional magazines have the same problem with every issue.

If the articles and notices for the parish publication have been written as inverted pyramids, the editor can simply do a cursory check of the last paragraphs in the story, cut them, and throw them away. That might be painful surgery—particularly if the writer and the editor are the same person—but it is the best way to make sure stories can be made to fit. And while those deleted paragraphs might have been interesting, since they are at the bottom end of a story written in the style of an inverted pyramid, the information included there is not essential and probably will not be missed.

This brings us to the importance of paragraphs in news stories. Essayists write by the rule that every paragraph introduces a new thought, and the paragraph will not end until that idea has been fleshed out in full. Journalists work with short sentences in short paragraphs, often only one sentence each, seldom more than two. This is because journalists know that their readers have been conditioned to read news and announcements fast. In newspapers and newsmagazines, the combination of material set in narrow columns (and thus, in shorter lines) with short paragraphs looks less foreboding and helps people read the material more quickly.

The short indention at the beginning of each paragraph and the partially blank line at the end of that same paragraph (sometimes called a widow) provide white space needed to break up the monotonous gray look of columns full of unbroken text. Some publications also use one blank line of space between each paragraph, but this is unnecessary and can distract from the cohesiveness of a story by making it look like the article is made up of many disjointed pieces.

Focusing on Future Tense

It is time to move to other aspects of good reporting that affect content. Start with tense. Future tense is always stronger than past tense in the effort to motivate people to be an active participant in any program.

Most stories in a periodic newsletter need to focus on the future. Reports of what is going to be happening in regular meetings of youth groups and women of the congregation are almost always more interesting and useful to readers than reports of what happened a month ago. Who served the coffee and cookies, what games were played, or the nature of the weather at the last meeting three weeks ago is not going to attract inactive members of the congregation to these organizations. The nature of the program and the qualifications of the personnel making the presentation at the next meeting might.

A by-product of this kind of reporting is that all groups in the congregation are required to plan details of every meeting and other activity at least two months in advance. With practice, that planning will be extended to include the entire year. Everyone expects, of course, that the further away the meeting is when the initial plan is completed, the more fine tuning will be necessary as the date gets closer.

On the other hand, some past activities and actions dare not be ignored and need to be reported. It is significant if the council approves a major renovation project for the education unit, or provides some energy-saving regulations, or recommends that the staff be enlarged by adding one more pastor. That kind of past action needs reporting. It also needs background information regarding why the council made such decisions and what the long-term implications are for the life and ministry of the congregation.

If the story is renovation, what is the timetable for approval by the congregation (if needed), the completion of architectural drawings, the date when bids will be submitted, and projected schedules for construction? How the money will be raised to fund the project is probably a separate story on its own.

If the story is a report on energy-saving initiatives, what are the new regulations, how much money are they expected to save, how are members of the congregation expected to help?

If the story centers on expansion of staff, why is the new person needed, what are the primary elements of the job description for the new employee, what is the procedure and timetable for finding that person and having him or her join the congregation's staff?

Dealing with Minutes

Some congregations insist that the minutes of every council meeting be included in the next issue of the newsletter. It is an understatement to say that minutes of meetings are not scintillating reading. The fact is, minutes are one of the most deadly forms of prose ever invented.

Good minutes follow a chronological form that by its very nature buries some of the most significant actions and deletes details of some of the most colorful discussion. Members of the council *have* to read them. Archivists and historians thrive on the important information that can be found in them. Other members of the congregation should not be expected to read them quite so intensely or find them quite so exciting.

Instead, the newsletter editor or reporter should look at each month's minutes, decide what actions have potential for major financial, theological, or operational change, and pull those items out for a separate news story. Maybe so much is happening that one council meeting will generate several news stories. More likely, one or two council actions can be highlighted in the lead paragraph of the report and less significant decisions can be included in a few summary paragraphs after the introductory phrase, "In other action(s) . . ."

The best reporting happens when the editor or reporter is invited to sit in on council meetings so that she has firsthand information. If the council talks about personnel problems or other material not ready for public debate, it can go into executive session and the editor or reporter can be dismissed for that part of the meeting.

If a congregation's traditions seem to require the publication of the council's monthly minutes—I know of at least one congregation where the constitution requires such a practice—try a compromise.

Start using the form of reporting minutes outlined above for the newsletter. Then post the minutes on a bulletin board in a hallway. Announce the new procedures in the first newsletter story when you initiate the change.

Then stand back and watch how many people actually stop and take the time to read those posted minutes. I guarantee that the number will be painfully small, particularly if a good job is done in reporting the essentials of the meeting in the parish newsletter. Then the council can be asked to offer an amendment to the constitution—eliminating the mandate to publish the minutes—at the next annual meeting.

Note that all the information that might be included in whatever story you write is developed on the basis of questions. And all of the significant questions that will uncover information are aimed at discovering answers to, and are some extension of, who, what, when, where, and why or how. The good reporter never assumes that anyone else knows anything about the subject being reported. If the reporter assumes total ignorance of the facts before the reader looks at the story, readers will have all their questions answered clearly and directly without any ambiguity when they finish reading the article. Furthermore, enough informed sources have been included in the story so that if unanswered questions still exist, the reader knows where to go for more complete responses.

In other words, the well-written story: (1) identifies individuals and groups so that the most recent newcomer will know who and what they are, (2) specifies meeting-place locations if necessary so that everyone can find them, (3) helps everyone to feel invited, and (4) makes sure no information is ambiguous.

Now that content, structure and organization of a news story have been discussed, it is time to think about some of the niceties of efficient and economical language. First, shorten sentences to the basic communication of nouns and verbs. Use adjectives and adverbs sparingly, if at all. Adjectives and adverbs are frequently subjective rather than objective judgments of what took place and the conditions under which the action happened. Good writing for parish newsletters and bulletins always strives for objectivity. Subjective descriptions take up space and introduce elements that can be turned controversial by some readers.

A Style Sheet Is Not a Luxury

All writing has a particular style. The style determines how the writer deals with such basic concerns as capitalization, forms and uses of names, use of titles, abbreviations, designation of dates and times, punctuation, forms of numbers, and other elements of written communication.

I encourage every congregation to develop its own consistent, clear, and concise style sheet (see appendix B) reflecting practices and policies of the parish. The style sheet gives guidance regarding a large group of questions, including: What words should be capitalized and what words should not? How should people be identified? What abbreviations are acceptable? What form should dates take?

A good style sheet for a congregation is also always a work in progress, changing with times and needs. What is important is not so much which style writers and editors assimilate for their own use, but the consistency with which that style is put into practice once it is adopted as the norm.

Here is how a style sheet can be developed for your congregation. You and everyone else who is writing material for any parish publication always works with a notepad by their keyboard. Even better, open a new networked file called "Style Sheet" that is available to everyone on the staff who works on a word processor. Whenever a question of usage comes up for you or anyone else who is doing any writing, you can consider the stylistic possibilities, note your preference for future reference, and use that form in the story you are writing and all other stories you will write in the future.

These are only a few of the many questions you will deal with. Should I use or not use certain abbreviations, and when? How should people be addressed and identified? How do you deal with second and third references to your congregation and other proper nouns? What is the best procedure regarding ordinal numbers in dates?

Punctuation problems should also be included. For instance, in a series of subjects separated by commas, do you include a comma before the "and" or "or" preceding the last item in the list? Either usage can be correct. Choose one.

Then all the people who have been working on communications projects meet and compare notes (or simply check the networked word processor file). What did each one decide to do with the usage problems they confronted? Why did they make the decision they did? Agree on what the best decision is for your congregation's publications and make that the style to be used consistently from that time forward.

Keep in mind that shorter is almost always better, so standard abbreviations will probably work best. A major exception, however, is the postal system's two-digit, all-caps abbreviations for states. Some of them are confusing and can be misinterpreted, and all of them are aesthetically ugly and stand out inordinately from the rest of the text. Use the longer form standard abbreviations for states instead.

An easier way to find an appropriate style for your congregation's written communication might be to purchase one of several stylebooks that are available and use it as a guide with whatever modifications seem to be necessary. Two in particular can be useful. The most formal is *The Chicago Manual of Style* (CMOS) (University of Chicago Press, 1993). I recommend the *Associated Press Stylebook and Libel Manual* (AP), (Cambridge, Mass.: Perseus Publishing, 2002), as a beginning point for parish publications primarily because it emphasizes the popular form readers have become acquainted with in their newspapers and newsmagazines. It recommends use of fewer capital letters and more abbreviations, both space savers for publications that often do not have enough room to hold all the material written to go into them. *Getting the Word Out,* however, demonstrates both styles as CMOS is used for the text and AP is used for the examples and appendices. (AP can be purchased for less than $20 at most bookstores or on the Web.)

Even after you have the stylebook, it would still be good to write out a simplified style sheet that will apply to your congregation's publications; that way, copies of the simplified style can be handed out to everyone who writes anything for any of the congregation's publications. What is most important about the written style in your congregation's publications is that it is consistent. Too many times, when reviewing a congregation's bulletins and newsletter, I find the names of months spelled out in one sentence and abbreviated one line below. Or, some people are always referred to only by first name; others are identified several times in the same story with both first and last name. Or the time of a meeting is referred to as "7:30 P.M. in the evening" (use P.M. or evening, but never both in the same sentence).

Omit letters that are not necessary. Nov. 1st does not need the "st." When people read dates, they automatically fill in the st, nd, rd, and th suffixes after ordinal numbers. In space-restricted parish publications, those two letters can sometimes add one more line.

Being Alert for "There" and "This" Problems

No matter what the style, two words should be avoided like the plague. The first is the word *there*. Consider what happens when that word opens a sentence: "There will be a meeting of the church council at 7:00 P.M. on Tuesday, May 7." Such usage always uses more words than necessary to say the same thing, and says it in one of the dullest and most passive ways possible. Consider this alternative: "The church council will meet at 7:00 P.M. on Tuesday, May 7."

Better, but it still doesn't engender much excitement regarding the meeting. Try this: "The pastor's salary will be the major item on the agenda when the church council holds its regular meeting at 7:00 p.m. on Tuesday, May 7." This will generate interest, and all the members of the congregation will be waiting to read the report of that meeting when it appears in the next newsletter.

Take a look at the following example showing "abuse" of the word *there*.

Board of Education:
August 8 there will be a short meeting after church. On the agenda will be material, S.S. teachers and "Kick-off Sunday" on September 12. For this event there will be a picnic. Board of Ed will furnish hamburger, hot dogs and buns; and the ice cream and cones. Please bring salads. The picnic will be on the west side of the church. We still need teachers and subs so please consider helping out.

Difficulties include:

- Use of a heading rather than a headline
- Beginning the article with a date
- Spelling out the names of months
- Multiple uses of "there will be" language
- Uncertainty about which event is "this event"
- Who is the "we" that needs teachers? Is it remotely feasible that the Board of Education might provide the hamburger and hot dogs without the buns?

Here is a possible rewrite that corrects some of the problems.

**Board of Education Meeting Aug. 8;
Kick-off Sunday Planned for Sept. 12**

Members of the United Methodist Board of Education will meet after church on Aug. 8 to finalize plans on curriculum materials, Sunday School teachers, and "Kick-off Sunday."

Teachers and substitutes are still needed for this fall, according to Marilyn Smarts, education board chair. She asked that anyone interested in being a teacher contact any members of the Board of Education soon. They are listed below with their phone numbers.

Kick-off Sunday on Sept. 12 will feature an outdoor picnic on the west side of the church. Each member family of the congregation is asked to bring a salad. The Board of Education will provide hamburgers, hot dogs, and ice cream cones.

The second word to avoid is *this*. Note its use in the second line of the original "Board of Education" example. Think of what usually happens when the word *this* shows up in print, most often at the beginning of a sentence. *This* is a slow-down word, a caution light. It always refers back to something that was written earlier in the story. But does it refer to the last proper or improper noun in the last sentence, or was it something in the last paragraph, or might it be something that was only inferred anywhere along the line? No matter how far back or how close the reference is, the reader has to slow down and work out the logistics to gain clarity before going on. The use of *this* is almost never a clear reference. At best, it is sloppy writing. At worst, it introduces ambiguity and confusion for the reader.

Eliminate that Cliché

Many of us use language so casually and become so familiar with colloquialisms and cliches that we take them for granted. We seldom take the time to look at the words we write, and ask: "Does that phrase have any meaning?" "Does it mean what we really want to say?" "Is it appropriate for use in the context I have created for it?"

Consider a few popular phrases that show up coast to coast in worship service guides every week and in parish newsletters every month. None of these phrases were made up. All of them continue to occur with embarrassing frequency in too many parish publications.

45

"In loving memory." Why do we feel so compelled to include "loving?" Does anyone place flowers in the chancel or on the altar because they hate the memory of the person being memorialized? Not likely. The word is unnecessary, and often stretches the announcement to gobble up one more precious line of cramped bulletin space.

"Wouldn't it be wonderful if . . ." Would it? Using those words will not make it so. On the other hand, if the story includes enough scintillating, objective details of a meeting that is coming up in two weeks, members of the prospective audience might say to themselves, "That sounds like a wonderful meeting. I'm marking it on my calendar so I won't miss it."

"It was an enjoyable, wonderful evening." Was it? The people who were there might agree—or might not. The people who were not there probably do not care. If the story that includes the subjective acclamation is reporting a significant event in the congregation, the report should include enough objective detail so that the reader says either: "It was an enjoyable, wonderful evening. I'm glad I participated" or "That sounds like an enjoyable evening. I'm sorry I didn't go."

"Why not come?" Ask a negative question; get a negative answer. Make the case for participation by the readers of your bulletin announcements or newsletter stories with program details that are irresistible, not easily dismissed clichés. A Bible study led by a 74-year-old saint of the congregation, a program presentation by a former member who is now an esteemed social worker, a hymn-sing led by the admired choir director, refreshments by three women who everyone recognize as the best cooks in the community, opportunities to become better acquainted with other people who have similar concerns and interests—those are potential reasons why people will want to be present. "Why not come?" will never be persuasive.

"I would like to take this opportunity to thank you." Go ahead. Those 10 words take up almost a full line in many bulletin formats. They can (and should) be replaced with two: "Thank you" or an even shorter "Thanks."

Never, ever begin or include within an article the poisonous phase, "As you know . . ." Inclusion of those words tells readers they do not have to spend anymore time with this material because they already know it. Maybe the information has already been stated at an earlier time in a prior publication. If that is so, fine. But do not tell the reader. Rearrange the paragraphs, add more recent developments, and rewrite the lead sentence. If readers say, "I already know this," and stop reading after a paragraph or two, that is their prerogative. Avoid giving them a head start on that decision by telling them up front that they already know it. Most likely they do not.

People do not always remember everything they have read or heard from month to month. Some communication and marketing surveys taken years ago discovered that most people need to hear or read something seven times before they really assimilate it as their own information.

Some news stories should show up in your parish newsletter three months in a row. But every time that story is published it must be different. Committees have met and changed or added to their initial decisions. The project is running either ahead or behind its initially announced timetable. Funding has been so successful that the project can be enlarged and enhanced, or funding has been disappointing and the project needs more support or has to be pared back. But never, through all of that reporting, should you use the words, "As you know."

Dealing with Those Pesky Pronouns

The need to write objectively has already been introduced. Objective language cuts out the editorial opinion of the writer and lets each reader make his own judgments in their response to the veracity and persuasiveness of the content of news stories and announcements. Nowhere does subjective communication create bigger problems than in the use of the first person plural pronouns "we," "us," and "our." It happens innocently enough. In an effort to give communication a warm and fuzzy inclusiveness, the writer slips into shoddy language that is neither clear nor inclusive. Consider the following example from a Sunday worship service guide:

> **MID-WEEK ADVENT SERVICES THIS WEDNESDAY.** This year, we will again be using the beautiful Holden Evening Prayer Service. Each week we will take a peek into the life of some of those people who are part of the Christmas Story. Plan to join us this Wednesday at 7:00 p.m. for the final mid-week Advent worship service.

First question: If the midweek Advent service being announced is the final one of the series, why is the item written as if it is introducing the beginning of the season?

Answer: A standard format probably had been set up for a series of four announcements in consecutive service guides. But no one thought to look at the text to see if it might benefit from a bit of weekly editing to make it more timely and appropriate.

Second question: Who are the "we" and the "us"?

Answer: The first and the second "we" could be the pastor, the pastoral staff, or the worshipers. The "us" could be the pastor, the pastoral staff, or those people who can be depended upon always to worship at midweek services.

Either way, the language is not inclusive, particularly for those people on the inactives and prospects lists. Think about the prospects for membership or the inactives in your congregation that you identified earlier in chapter 3. They look at the "we" and "us" in the item above—the language that was so casually inserted to be so intimate and inclusive—and they say, "I'm not really a part of that group. That invitation is for those who already are attending and actively involved."

The intention for inclusiveness has been turned on its head. Instead, some readers—the readers your congregation really wants and needs to reach—find such subjectivity a language of exclusiveness. That is an interpretation that, rightly or wrongly, makes your congregation seem to them like an exclusive closed club and cuts them off from either renewing or beginning the fellowship in mission that both they and the congregation covets.

If a "we" refers to a leadership group, avoid the subjective pronoun and name the group. The first usage would be the church council, the worship planning committee, or the parish education committee. Subsequent uses in the same story would reference the council or the committee.

If "us" refers to an entire congregation, give the proper name of the congregation the first time (e.g., First Baptist Church), then use synonyms throughout the rest of the story—the congregation, the church, the worshipers, the gathering, the group, and so forth.

If the "we" is an audacious "royal we" referring to the pastor and used instead of the singular first person pronoun "I," name the pastor the first time (e.g., Pastor Luther Jones). Later uses in the same story refer to Pastor Jones or "the pastor."

Let's try a different approach to the midweek Advent service announcement above:

LAST MID-WEEK ADVENT SERVICE WEDNESDAY, DEC. 22. The lives of the shepherds who went to Bethlehem to worship the Christ child will be the focus of the final mid-week Advent Service on Wednesday. The liturgical setting will be Holden Evening Prayer Service. Worship begins at 7:00 p.m.

Check the changes: The item has been tailored to its place in the four-part series. It states the facts clearly in objective terms, and anyone who reads it will know exactly who is being referred to and will not feel excluded by the subjective and noninclusive "we" and "us" language.

The writers of the ubiquitous "Welcome" included in most worship service guides are too often sucked into the same subjective language trap as if it were quicksand. Consider:

WELCOME TO OUR VISITORS! We're glad you're here. We invite you to have a cup of coffee with us between our services. Please sign our guest book as you leave the Sanctuary and fill in one of the yellow cards if we can be of any service to you. It's good to have you with us.

Note that the language in the "Welcome" is not only exclusive, but it has also become possessive: "our visitors," "our services," and "our guest book." The matter of identification also gets a bit murky. Who is the "we're" who is glad "you're" here? Who is inviting the visitors to coffee? Who is the "us" "it's good to have you with"? Perhaps a different approach would work better.

Welcome to worship at First Presbyterian. Visitors and members are invited to become better acquainted over a cup of coffee in Fellowship Hall between services. Visitors are asked to sign the guest book as they leave the sanctuary. Anyone wanting special ministry is asked to fill in one of the yellow cards in the pew racks and place it in the offering plate.

The possessiveness is gone. In its place is more substantive information regarding the location of the coffee, where to find the yellow cards and what to do with them, all questions to which most visitors need answers. Even the name of the church was included.

Remember, you cannot assume that anyone knows anything about what you are writing except yourself—particularly when you are targeting inactive members and visitors. And one more thing: note that the lead sentence has been changed to boldface only. In the original example, three means of emphasis—boldface, all caps, and underlined—were used at the same time. That is graphic overkill and is unnecessary. It's a problem that will be explored in the next chapter.

A close cousin to the we, us, and our problem is the use of the word *you*. *You* becomes particularly problematic when it is followed by should, must, will, and other imperatives which invariably produce a carping and whining sound that backs people into a corner and might even raise the specter of guilt. While your congregation knows about guilt—and forgiveness—the concept in this context is not particularly productive and even causes some people to dig in their heels and say a simple but emphatic no.

Empowering the Subjective Voice

But sometimes you want the voice of subjectivity. Sometimes the facts of the story need to be bolstered by personal opinions that reflect—even emphasize—the personal feelings of church staff and other members. It takes more time and more work, but a few short interviews, often over the phone, will garner opinions, emotions, and sensitivities about schedule changes, building plans, stewardship drives, and evangelism emphases that a congregation is planning or, in some cases, has already implemented.

Sources for such interviews in addition to the pastor include committee chairs, older members, newer members, younger members, and expert "witnesses" in the congregation who are professionally involved in similar concerns. When these varied opinions are incorporated in the story, they are in quotes, they are attributed to the person by name, and the person is identified in specific terms. The quotation can, and probably should, include all of the subjective language the source brought to bear when he was being interviewed. Good quotations can overflow with emotion, always within the boundaries of quotation marks. Using a quote is also one way of dealing with people who think too highly of their own writing.

Nearly every congregation has at one time or another had the problem of dealing with the organization "reporter" who has convinced herself (sometimes with the help of friends) that she is a great writer. She submits articles for the newsletter or bulletin on a regular basis, almost always with the caveat, "You need to use this, and I don't want one thing changed." Most of these people have seldom heard of the five W's, the idea of writing in an inverted pyramid is totally foreign, and they love their subjective language. Their sense of what is important for the reading audience focuses on the past, including the weather and the color of the Jell-O served with the refreshments. Their orientation to the minutia of the past seldom allows them to think in terms of the next program. You know that including their article will downgrade the quality of everything else in the publication and will not inform people about future programs in the way that is needed. What can you do? Several things.

First, hold a workshop sponsored by the congregation's public relations committee, council, or pastoral staff (more about parish public relations committees in chapter 7), in which basic rules of writing for the parish publications are spelled out and practiced. It would be best, however, if such a workshop did not happen until after your congregation has conducted its own self-study and analysis (see chapter 3 and appendix A). Some larger congregations might even consider hiring a professional communicator to conduct a comprehensive publications or public relations audit, which critiques both the philosophy and the practice of the congregation's entire communications program.

If such an audit is in the future, tell the person who submits the questionable article that the best thing every writer needs (and professional writers know this well) is a good editor. (Editors also know that the best thing they need is good writers.) Indicate that some changes might have to be made so that the writing style is consistent throughout the publication.

While the person delivering the piece is still in the office, glance at it and ask questions that will supply answers to whatever essential information is missing. Who is the featured speaker at the next meeting? What are her credentials? Is the program offering anything out of the ordinary? Is a Bible study or worship program included? Who is leading it? Are date, time, and place included and correct?

Once the person who delivered it has left the office, take the piece that has been offered and rework it to include the facts you uncovered in that brief interview. But what do you do with all that subjective fluff that permeated the initial article? You have two options. First, simply eliminate all of that subjective material. But you know that you do that at your peril. Your editing will not be appreciated, and in the process you might cut off a significant source of important information for future activities.

Second, revise the original article, adding those substantive facts you learned while talking to the original author. As for the subjective fluff, gather the best of it together in one or two quotes, attribute the quotation(s) to the person who brought the material to your office, and give her an identity that might range all the way from president to secretary to special reporter.

When people are quoted, particularly when the quote infers a certain position of leadership, they often feel that they have been bestowed with added and significant status. When you put quotation marks around something they have said or written, and credit them by name and title as the source, it takes most of the sting out of having the article they submitted substantially rewritten.

Let's look at one more example.

BIG NEWS

COME TO THE PARTY

Are you ready to have some FUN? Could you spare some time for FELLOWSHIP? Are your willing to help our church do some intentional planning for the FUTURE?

You can do all of the above if you attend the Long-Range Planing Party on Friday, October 30 from 7 to 9:15 p.m. and Saturday, October 31, from 9 a.m. to 4 p.m. Not only will you enjoy yourself at this get-together, but you will learn a lot and be a great assistance to your church.

When we are done on Saturday afternoon, our congregation will have two or three specific goals for the future that will significantly improve our mission and ministry. These will be well-thought-out goals and ones which CAN and WILL be accomplished beginning the very next day.

Sounds great, doesn't it!!! Our planning party theme will be "New Vision/New Harvest". There will be decorations galore and a few people (perhaps our 12 Keys Steering Committee members dressed to suit the occasion).

We'll be taking reservations soon. Please mark your calendars and plan on taking part. Please note, any confirmed member may participate . . . young people are invited, too! You'll be hearing more details soon. Thanks.

Big News has big problems. The rewrite below solves most of them.

Long Range Planning Party to Involve All Members Oct. 30-31

Every member of Gethsemane Lutheran Church is invited to be part of a major planning process to set goals for the congregation's ministry for the next five years.

"New Vision/New Harvest," is the theme for the two-day long-range planning party on Friday and Saturday, Oct. 30-31.

The Friday meeting will begin at 7:00 and end at 9:15 p.m. The Saturday session will run from 9:00 a.m. until 4:00 p.m. The church council will provide a free lunch for all participants on Saturday.

Cliff Johnson, council president and chair of the steering committee for the event, said, "When we are done on Saturday afternoon, our congregation will have two or three specific goals for the future that will significantly improve our mission and ministry. These will be well-thought-out goals and ones which can and will be accomplished beginning the very next day."

All confirmed members, including the congregation's youth, are encouraged to attend. Childcare services will be provided for younger families.

"Not only will participants of all ages enjoy themselves at this get-together," said Pastor John Anderson, "but they will learn a lot about their congregation and the church at large while helping in the essential work of planning the future of Gethsemane."

The steering committee will be enhancing the "party atmosphere" of the event with decorations, and some will be dressed in costume.

Call the church office (123-4567) by Oct. 27 to make your reservations.

Getting Tense about Tense

Tense is important when dealing with announcements. For instance, when someone wrote, "Thank you to the following who have helped with today's service," she was locked into the past tense mode for a present tense activity. The announcements in most worship service guides are expected to be read before or (perish the thought) during the service.

If that's the case, the correct tense for that little announcement is present perfect and the item should read: "Thank you to the following who are helping with today's service."

The difficulty appears most often when acknowledging the work of volunteers during a service—ushers, readers, cantors, the choir, acolytes. Write the acknowledgment several days before the service. Always keep in mind the conjunction between when the reader sees the information and when the volunteer is doing the service, and write the tenses accordingly.

Playing with Punctuation

Too many faith group offices have equipment that needs upgrading. The problem might be called the "stuttering keyboard," and it rears its ugly head in problems with punctuation. Exclamation points, for example, work well only when they are used as rarities. Seldom does objective reporting call for or allow an exclamation point. But they run rampantly through many parish publications as though they were the ultimate answer to getting a reader's attention and response.

Rather than emphasizing the content of a sentence through its language and context, a vast number of writers drop exclamation points into their prose as though this mark alone will get people excited. Even worse, too often a parish publication writer looks at the exclamation point they have put in place, decides the emphasis is not strong enough, and calmly adds two or four more with their stuttering keyboard. I recently saw a newsletter article that was submitted with 47 exclamation points after what was supposed to be a headline. That is a new and unfortunate record (see chapter 8).

Or sometimes, if the writer thinks three exclamation points are insufficient, he or she concocts a combination of exclamation points and question marks such as "!?!?!?!". Such forms of punctuation have never existed in the lexicon of good writing. Do not try to create them. A single exclamation point or a single question mark do their jobs all by themselves. If you use them at all, allow them to stand alone.

Another mangling of the rules happens with simple periods. One period ends a sentence. Three periods, known as an ellipsis, indicates that a word or words has been left out of a quotation. Four periods indicate that something has been omitted at the end of a sentence (the ellipsis plus the necessary period). That's it. Correct usage never includes five, six, or nine periods in a row. The AP Stylebook does not ever recognize anything besides a period and an ellipsis as correct punctuation.

Going Proactive with Headlines

Perhaps you are wondering about references above to the insufficiency of headings as opposed to headlines. Too many parish newsletters settle for one or two words—often centered and in boldface or all caps or a combination of both—at the top of a story that simply identifies the general subject matter or the committee or organization involved. Such beginning points are called headings. They are words such as: "Stewardship," "Evangelism," "Building Fund," "Potluck Dinner," "Education Program," "Ski Trip," "Swimming Party," "Help Needed," "Council Meeting," and a hundred other topics.

What happens if you are one of the people in the target audience and a newsletter article begins with those words? If the subject sounds like it could be of interest to you, you might begin to read the article to see how important the information is. If, on the other hand, you think the subject has no significance for you, or if you really do not wish to know anything else about it because you are a little tired of "Stewardship," "Evangelism," or "Education Program," and think you probably know what the story is going to say anyway, and you would just as soon not be involved, it's likely you will pass by the article completely. That's the danger of headings. But try a headline in a heading's place.

A headline is written to attract interest and readership. It is a succinct condensation of most of the five W's in the story that follows. It has a subject and an object. A verb might be included, but it can also be implied. Articles (a, an, the) can be left out, and you can use your discretion regarding the inclusion of conjunctions (and, but, or, etc.).

Headlines stop readers at the top of the story and invite—no, urge—them to read the story to learn, assimilate, and act upon the information. Headlines are usually in boldface type and are set bigger than the text of the story. Depending on the placement of the story in the newsletter, the headlines might be one line across two or three columns (for the major story on the page) or two or three lines of approximately the same length in one column.

Headlines almost always read best when flush left rather than centered, and all lines are nearly equal in length. Avoid any usage where a two- or three-line headline ends with only one short word on the last line. It's simply aesthetically not as pleasing as lines of more equal length.

Here's how it works. Perhaps the heading is:

EDUCATION

The headline might be

**New Sunday School
Curriculum to Be
Introduced in Fall**

Perhaps the heading is:

COUNCIL

The headline might be:

Parking Lot Paving Approved by Council

or, if you need a shorter version:

Council Approves Paving Parking Lot

or, shorter yet:

Council OKs Parking Lot Paving

Perhaps the heading is:

YOUTH

The headline might be:

Ten Teens Travel to Kentucky
To Help Appalachian Families

Notice the difference? Headlines will beat headings hands down every time when it comes to triggering reader interest and helping them to get involved in the story. Do not let potential readers off the hook by letting them think they already know what is under a heading and do not need or want to know the facts of the story that follows. Draw them into the story with an active headline. Then make sure the story includes answers to all five W's with objective language that is both interesting and challenging.

One more thing. Only the editor writes headlines because only the editor knows where the story will go in the newsletter, how it will fit the format, and how strong an emphasis it needs to have in relation to the other stories in the publication. Headline writing is an art. It takes practice. But it is also fun. Enjoy working on it.

Conclusion

Plain and simple objective language that includes all the necessary details of any cause or event allows people to think through the facts, check their calendars, and say, "That sounds like an interesting program, and I want to be part of that activity." And they will.

Readability is central to understanding and action. If the material in your bulletin and newsletter is readable—full of facts and unencumbered by subjectivity—it will also be remembered. The more readable the information, the more likely it will be read and remembered. And the more information is remembered, the more likely it will motivate people to act.

5

Designing a Format That Fosters Readability

The following chapter includes multiple notations intended to help parish publications editors find their way around the functions on their word processors so that they might enjoy themselves more in their creative work of writing, editing, and designing their congregation's communications tools.

Since I have used only a PC rather than a Macintosh ever since I gave up my electric typewriter about a quarter century ago, the detailed computer functions I pass on in this and other chapters are based only on work with a PC loaded with Windows 98.

Mac users should be able to find and use most of the functions itemized in Getting the Word Out *(even though they might be defined with other terminology). If you are working with a Mac, check your word processor's help menus, software manuals, and other resource books for routing through most of the same kinds of procedures (and a few that a PC does not offer).*

No matter whether you use a PC or a Mac, take time to experiment. Look at every function in each drop-down menu and learn what it will help you accomplish. Note the built-in redundancies and try them all to see which set of functions suites you best. Be confident. It's almost impossible to lose something, and you can nearly always reclaim the material in its previous form. But most of all, enjoy the blessings of what you and your word processor can create together.

One resource to help PC users unlock the marvelous mysteries that abound in their word processors is Andy Rathbone's Windows 98 for Dummies *(Foster City, Calif.: IDG Books Worldwide, 1998). Similar books within the Dummies series have been published for the Macintosh operating system.*

No matter how polished the prose, no matter how persuasive the facts, no matter how disciplined the objectivity, they are all for naught if the words do not attract the reader's eyes to the page and hold him there. Only the core of your congregation's audience (with perhaps a small percentage of the muscle) will take the time and the energy to struggle through words piled too thick, too small, too buried, too garbled in decorative type to attract and hold the reader until he has harvested all the information you have planted.

Readable publication design starts with three unassailable facts. If the lines are too long, if the type is too small, if the type face is too hard to read, the publication will be relegated to somewhere near the bottom of that competitive pile of print in the mailbox. Remember the challenges of competition in chapter 1? Here—at the point of format and design—is where your parish publications face their toughest test.

Line Length Critical Factor

Start with the length of the printed line of type. Many studies dealing with the readability of different kinds of type faces and the optimum length of printed lines were popular in the middle of the 20th century. Results of readership surveys done every 10 years by the Missouri School of Journalism, University of Missouri–Columbia, were published in the "Shop Talk at Thirty" column of *Editor and Publisher,* a weekly magazine aimed specifically at journalists, advertising agencies, and other communicators. Unfortunately, those surveys stopped several decades ago.

However, similar information on readability and how it applies to improved publication writing and design is included often in communications newsletters such as *The Ragan Report* and *Communications Briefings.* (For more information about either newsletter try www.ragan.com or www.briefings.com. Both Web sites introduce a variety of subscription newsletters that congregations might find useful.)

The readability surveys demonstrate consistently that the length of a line of type has a great deal to do with how easily material in a publication can be read and remembered. The formula that came out of those surveys works like this:

The length of line that produces optimum readability is one and one-half lowercase alphabets in letters and spaces. That's 26 (one alphabet) plus 13 (one-half an alphabet) equaling a total of 39 letters and spaces. People have good readability with lines up to two lowercase alphabets in length (52 letters and spaces), and down to one lowercase alphabet (26 letters and spaces).

However, when line length goes past two lowercase alphabets in length (52 letters and spaces), readability literally "drops off the table." Going the other way, readability decreases markedly when line length drops below one lowercase alphabet (26 letters and spaces).

The genius of this readability formula is that its holds true regardless of what size of type is used. As the size of the type gets larger (or smaller), the length of a readable line increases (or decreases) proportionately. The formula remains the same.

Consideration of Typesize Is Essential

The size of the type is the second major factor in readability. All of us know about "reading the small print" in contractual arrangements. People sometimes get in trouble when they skip that part because it is just too much work and takes too much time to read. If the letters are too small, most people have trouble reading the material without the help of a magnifying glass. To further complicate the problem, much of the small type encountered is in lines much too long to read easily, even when individual letters and words can be identified.

For instance, if your congregation's newsletter is printed vertically on 8½ by 11 inch paper and the margins are three-fourths of an inch on each side, a single line of 12 point Times New Roman type will include nearly 100 letters and spaces—about double the length of a readable line. That page should be designed in at least two, and preferably three, columns to have any chance of being readable. (For examples, see appendix C: Demonstrations in Readability.)

Choice of Font Fun But Fundamental

The readability of type is further complicated by the design of the letters. Your word processor probably came with upwards of 225 different type designs. Your computer refers to all typestyles or faces as "fonts" (see appendix D: Type Specimen List). Note that some fonts include only one or two styles (regular and boldface). Some fonts include only capital letters. Other fonts include whole families of type (light, regular, bold, italic, bold italic, condensed, condensed bold, etc.). They are just lying there at your disposal, begging to be used.

Out of that colorful list, however, less than 20 type families are easily read. The others include too many flourishes, too bold a line, and attempts to be too cute and too clever to be used at all except in a short (three to nine words) introductory phrase, or perhaps as a large, ornamental initial letter.

The study of type is fascinating, and the right selection can set a mood for an article or give hints regarding content simply by the style of its face. Unless you are really familiar and knowledgeable about all of your typeface options, however, you could spend hours making type choices that probably are not worth all the time they take. The choices might even be counterproductive, as they distract from the content.

Making the Serif, Sans Serif Decision

All type is divided into two basic categories: serif and sans serif. Serifs are the little "feet" or "ears" extending from the bottoms and tops of all the letters in the alphabet, whether they are capitals or lowercase. Believe it or not, those little serifs actually help the reader to stay on the line. And the longer the line, the more important they are for readability. Serif lightface typestyles are always the most readable (another fact proven consistently by readability studies).

Of the font families shown in appendix D, only Adobe Garamond, Bernhard, Book Antiqua, Bookman Old Style, Calisto MT, Century Schoolbook, Garamond, Goudy, Palatia, Paramount, Perpetua, Roman, Times and Times New Roman, and Windsor are readable serif faces.

The typefaces available in families (lightface, boldface, italic, expanded, condensed and a few other specialties thrown in for the fun of it) provide the most natural variations. It is best to use one or two of those families for your parish publications, simply because they offer more options. (More about that appears later in this chapter in the section, "Dealing with the Possibilities of Emphasis.")

If a font shows a family of only one face, you can make your own family by using the "B" (bold) and "I" (italic) icons on your word processor toolbar. However, that often is too cumbersome to be a good option for large blocks of text.

Given all of the factors spelled out above, the Times New Roman family is one of the most readable choices for parish publications.

Sans serif fonts are type styles without serifs. They do not have any of the miniscule "feet" and "ears" to guide the reader along the line, and they are often called block letters. Consequently, although the reader has every intention of keeping her eyes on the line started on the left-hand edge of the page, without those little guides the eyes begin to wander. The longer the line, the more the wandering, so at the end, the eyes are fighting to stay on the line they started on. That fight slows down and confuses the reader. Sans serif fonts can be useful in short blocks such as headlines, headings, subheads, call outs, and introductory text, but avoid using them in long blocks of text.

Among the more readable sans serif font families in appendix D are Arial, Continuum, Eras, Franklin, Helv, Helvetica, Lucinda Sans, News Gothic, Quick, System, and VAG Rounded.

Some people look at all those typefaces available at the touch of their fingers to their word processor keyboard, and their responses go back to the feelings they had when they were kids in a candy store. "I have so many typographical goodies that I can't decide which I like best," they say, "so I'll just sample a whole lot of them."

And, unfortunately, they do. Six or seven or more typefaces decorate every page of their newsletters. The fonts fight each other aesthetically. Readers, finding no consistency, are forced into the unpalatable problem of adjusting their vision to pick up all the different goodies, and eventually give up entirely and say that maybe they do not need to know this information anyway.

Back in the candy store, too much of all those good things sometimes made the sampler sick. In a parish newsletter, too many of those unpalatable typefaces make a potential reader into a distressed nonreader. A good rule of thumb is never to use more than three fonts in the same parish publication. Limiting your choices to two readable fonts is even better. A relatively common combination is to use a serif font such as Times New Roman for all of the text, and a sans serif font such as Helvetica Bold for all heads and headings. It works just as well, however, to use only Times New Roman (or a similar serif type face) for everything in the publication—lightface (also referred to as roman or regular face) for the text and boldface for the heads.

Typesize Is a Basic Readability Decision

Another decision that needs to be made involves the size of type. Type-sizes have been standardized since 1737 when Pierre Simon Fournier developed the first successful system based on a unit of size called a point. The United States Typefounders Association officially adopted the point system in 1886.

Your word processor, with all of its modern technology, retains the ancient point system in its measurement and designation of the fonts available for your use. Twelve points make up one pica. You can set the default on your computer to the pica measurement rather than inches if you want. A pica is about one-sixth of an inch, making a point one-seventy-second of an inch. In other words, a point is a measurement only as big as the width of a couple of hairs laid side by side. Point is abbreviated as pt., and that is the designation that will be used from now on in this book.

The text of a story in most of your parish publications should be at least 10 pt., although 11 or 12 pt. is better. Of course, the larger the typesize, the more space an article will take in the publication and the less space you have for more articles. The trade-off is better readability versus more space for content. A good combination is 10 pt. Times New Roman type for the text, with headlines in 12 to 24 pt. bold Times New Roman or Helvetica, depending on the length and impor-tance of the story.

If the story is only a two-paragraph (maximum of four sentences) announcement, the headline—probably one line—would be 12 or 14 pt. bold in one column. If the story is the major story on the first page and deals with the implementation of a new program in the congrega-tion, it probably needs a head that would cross over at least two of the three columns in two lines of 18 pt. bold type or one line of 20 or 24 pt. bold.

What is known as the "x factor" also has a bearing on your choice of type. Most of the letters in the alphabet—all lowercase vowels except *i* and the consonants *c, m, n, r, s, v, w, x,* and *z* have the same standard height in a line of the same size type. Other letters such as *b, d, f, h, i, k, l,* and *t* are ascenders. That means part of the letter extends above the standard height—the x factor—of the line. Other letters

63

such as *g, j, p, q,* and *y* are descenders. Parts of those letters drop below the standard depth of the line.

A 12 pt. line is measured from the top of the highest ascender (they are not necessarily all the same height) to the bottom of the lowest descender. The lowercase letters without ascenders or descenders make up the measurement of the "x factor." Some typefaces are designed with shorter ascenders and descenders. Those faces will always look bigger when compared with same size faces with longer ascenders and descenders.

Look again at the list of type specimens in appendix D. All the sample typefaces on those pages are 12 pt. In other words, as far as typography is concerned, they are the same size. The depth of their line takes up the same amount of space. But notice how much smaller some of them look. In particular, study Abadi MT Condensed, Bavand, Bernhard Modern, Christie, Cotillion, Diner, Franciscan, French Script, Gill Sans MT, Gloucester MT, Invitation, Litterbox, Mariah, NewZurica, Nuptial Script, Park Avenue, Perpetua, Quill, Sniff, TypoUpright, and Zelda.

If you have a hard time reading the sample in the Type Specimens List, then do not even think about trying to use that font in your parish publications. Someone designed each of those typefaces with a specific purpose in mind. But sometimes that purpose was and is extremely limited and was never intended for use in a parish bulletin or newsletter. In fact, when you look at some of them, you have to wonder why anyone ever went to the trouble of designing them at all.

Line Spacing Is Also Significant

The space between the lines of type also affects readability. If two or more lines of type have no space between them, and an ascender and a descender happen to end up exactly above and below one another, the ascender and descender actually touch. Imagine what that does to readability in a large block of text, and you know that font needs to have space between the lines.

People who are professional printers always talk about type as 10 on 11, 10 on 12, 10 on 13, and so forth. They might even make a reference to 10 on 11½. Thin as one point is, it can be divided into halves in typography. The printer is referring to 10 pt. type on 11 pt., 11½ pt., 12 pt., or 13 pt. lines of space.

A limited amount of space between lines increases readability. However, too much space between lines, such as adding a full line or more of white space between every line of type (for instance, 12 on 24 pt.), detracts from readability by making each line stand alone rather than as an integrated part of a united piece of text. The usual spacing for good readability is two points of space between lines (12 on 14 pt.).

Generally, if the type you select and use consistently in your parish publication is 11 pt., the technical terminology used to designate it is "11 pt. solid" (no space between the lines), or "11 on 12 pt.," "11 on 14 pt.," and so forth. More about line spacing and how you can control it appears later in this chapter in the section headed "Dealing with the Possibilities of Emphasis."

Be aware that line spacing is also a tricky decision. You need a small amount of space between lines for good readability, but the more space you have between lines the less space you have for content.

Using Your Word Processor Creatively for Typography

Your word processor allows you to change fonts, typesizes, and line spacing easily. All word processing programs have similar symbols and icons across two or three lines called toolbars at the top of your monitor. Usually, one toolbar will include "Body Text" or "Normal," the name of a font, a number, **B**, *I*, <u>U</u>, and four boxes filled with series of short horizontal lines.

All toolbars have similarities, but not all toolbars are the same. Instructions here are tied to the PC Windows 98 toolbars illustrated in these pages. If you are working with other programs or different computers, you might have to adapt the instructions to make them fit the toolbars on your word processor.

If you click your mouse once on the arrow (a little triangle with the point down) to the right of the "Style" window, a menu will drop down that allows you to preset (default) typestyles and sizes for body text of documents as well as several different headings, footers, headers, and page numbers.

The second box in the toolbar deals with fonts. After you have highlighted a block of text, click once on the little upside-down triangle on the right, and you can scroll down through a list of all the fonts available in your word processor. The ones you have used most recently will be separated out at the top of the list. Choose the one you want, click on it once, and that will be the typeface for the text high-lighted on your screen and whatever additional text you write immedi-ately following the highlight.

The next box holds a number. Click once on the arrow to the right of the number (or, if the box is blank, where the number should be) and you have a listing of all the typesizes available in your computer. Choose the one you want for the bulk of your text.

If you want to see the style and form of every letter in a given font, click once on "Start" (a button at the bottom left corner of your moni-tor), click once on "Programs," click on "Accessories," click on "Sys-tem Tools," and finally click on "Character Map." Character Map shows you the form and style of every letter (cap and lower case) for every font you have in your computer and is a great aid in choosing readable faces. (The Macintosh equivalent for Character Map is "Key Caps," which is found in the Apple Menu.)

It also includes all the symbols, dingbats, and diacritical marks (accents such as ê, ç, or ø used in foreign languages) available in that face. Every font in the Windows Character Map has all the diacritical marks available in that typeface for any language that uses English let-ters. (Some other programs might not have them all.)

The Character Map is also a great place to pick up a variety of styles of boxes if you are putting together a form where people are expected to check off their preferences. To pick up any of these special features, highlight the one you want by clicking on it once, then go to the boxes at the upper right, click on "Select," click on "Copy," click on "Close." That puts the typographical feature on your word proces-sor clipboard.

Now go back to your original text, put your cursor where you want the item from the Character Map to be placed, and click on "Paste," either in the toolbar, two icons to the right of the scissors, or in the "Edit" menu. ("Paste" will probably be represented by an icon that looks like a clipboard with a loose piece of paper.)

You can now paste the chosen symbol wherever else you might want it until you go back to the Character Map and choose something else. You can also change the size by simply highlighting the symbol where you have placed it, go up to the typesize window in the toolbar at the top of the monitor, and pick the size you want it to be. Most of the time, you will want the imported symbol to be the same size as the text. It is easy, however, to make it either larger or smaller.

The three boldfaced letters to the right of typesize on the toolbar represent Bold (**B**), Italic (*I*), and Underline (U). Highlight any word, phrase, clause, sentence, or paragraph of any text, click once on any one or a combination of those three letters, and your text will be changed to that form. Click on any of those letters again while the text is still highlighted, and it will return to its original form.

Dealing with the Possibilities of Emphasis

Your word processor makes at least three types of text emphasis as easy as a couple of flicks of your fingers. Highlight a letter, a word, a phrase, a sentence, or a paragraph, and click on **B**, *I*, or U, and you have immediately made those letters boldface or italic, or have underlined the highlighted section. Or, if you are dealing with an extended block of text, simply choose the boldface or italic style of type from the family you are working with.

Or, if you want your text in all caps, and it was not typed that way originally, click on "Format" at the top of the toolbar and drop down to "Change Case." You have five choices. "Sentence case" gives you a capital first letter, a period at the end, and everything in between in lowercase. You have to handle capitalization of proper nouns separately. But be careful (see the fifth and sixth pages of appendix C starting on page 222). Note your own experience when you read those paragraphs printed in all caps. Readability is bad enough when using the serif face at the bottom of the page, but it is nearly hopeless with the sans serif face at the top. Many churches put the congregational responses in the worship guide in all caps, which is not user friendly.

The reason type in all caps is hard to read is quite logical. When reading blocks of text, fast readers do not read by the letter, they read by the word—or even large groups of words. People who have taken speed-reading classes learn to read by seeing whole lines and groups of lines in one glance.

In order to identify words quickly, readers look for their "skyline"—the configuration of letters with ascenders and descenders.

When the word is printed in all caps, that "skyline" is taken away and the reader has to slow down to put the word together letter by letter.

Use the word *right* as an example. In lowercase, the word starts with one "x factor" letter, moves to the small ascender *i*, follows with a descender, and ends with two ascenders. Put the word *right* in all caps, however, and every letter is the same height: RIGHT. Readers have to slow down to put all those letters together in the word they need to read.

In addition, any word in all caps in a block of text automatically stands out from the material around it and provides a non-aesthetic blip that draws more attention than it usually deserves.

Every form of "emphasis" added to regular type decreases readability. Boldface, with its wider stroke, makes each letter and word more difficult to define. Italic, which deforms each letter from its usual pattern by slanting it to the right, does the same thing. Reverse, where letters come through as the color of the paper in a darker block of ink, are the most difficult of all.

Yet each of these forms has appropriate uses in small doses. A few boldface words give immediate emphasis to that phrase. Italic is the appropriate type style to use for titles of books, plays, and some other references to creative works. A small block of reverse type calls special attention to that content. However, it should usually be used as introductory material or as a call out rather than be inserted in the middle of an otherwise normal section of text.

The key is to be aware of the degree of difficulty that you add for the reader, and that you do not overwork forms of emphasis. If too much is emphasized, the impact is diluted and nothing is emphasized.

When you use various means of emphasis in text, use those emphases with economy. If you are using all caps, do not also use boldface. If a word is in boldface, it should not also be in italic. If it is in italic, it should not also be underlined. (Actually, those two forms of emphasis mean the same thing.)

In the worst case of emphasis overload I have ever seen, one church led off every announcement in the bulletin with a few words of boldface, all cap type (a procedure I recommend). However, the person doing this bulletin also underlined all the boldface lead-ins (completely unnecessary), and then, to make sure nobody missed it, added a boldfaced asterisk (*) before each boldface and underlined lead in. That asterisk did nothing except take up space.

One exception in doubling up emphasis is the use of boldface when a block of type is reversed. The thicker boldface makes a more open line when reversed, thus helping readability.

Back to your word processor's toolbar.

Four diagrams just to the right of center in your toolbar deal with line format. Highlighting a block of type and clicking on the first diagram will give you ragged right text. Clicking on the second diagram gives you a format where every line is centered. The third is ragged left, and the fourth is for justified text. More about those formatting options later in this chapter in the section titled "Ragged Right or Justified?"

Changing the space between lines is relatively easy. Highlight one or two paragraphs of text where you want to check out spacing options. Go to the top of the listing at the top of the toolbar and click once on "Format." The first option in the drop down menu is "Font" which allows you to make changes in font and size similar to what you can do using the toolbar.

The second option when you click on "Format" is "Paragraph." Click that once and you have two folders named "Indents and Spacing" and "Line and Page Breaks." Click on "Indents and Spacing."

The second section deals with "Indentation." On the left-hand half of that section you can set the parameters for indenting sections of text to make them stand out from the main body of material. Note that the options are available in tenths of an inch. On the right-hand half of the section you can set the length of the indention for the first line of a paragraph.

The third section of the "Indents and Spacing" folder deals with space between lines or blocks of type. Boxes on the left side provide options to add space before and after every paragraph, an appropriate consideration for some forms of correspondence.

Boxes on the right side deal first with standard single space, space and a half, double space, and so forth in formatting any text being written. If you click on "Exactly" toward the bottom of that dropdown menu, you can then move your cursor to the box next to it on the right and indicate "exactly" how many points you want between each line.

Page Format Finalizes Typography

Formats vary almost as much as the number of parishes that develop them. Most of them start with one of two sizes of paper—letter (8½ by

11 inches) and legal (8½ by 14 inches). Barring truly unusual folds, those sizes translate into six possibilities for the size of a single page. Keep in mind that all formats with a fold automatically have a minimum of four pages, and additions must be made in either four-page components or two-page components (front and back). If you use a full-size sheet of paper as your basic one-page format, you automatically have two pages (front and back) and can add pages in increments of two.

Paper that is 8½ by 11 inches can be used in pages of that size (front and back), or it can be folded into four 8½ by 5½ inch pages (the standard size for most worship service guides). It can also be folded into four 11 by 4¼ inch pages (the proportion is improved aesthetically if this strong vertical format is trimmed to 9 or 9½ inches tall).

Paper of 8½ by 14 inches can be used in pages that size, or it can be folded into four 8½ by 7 inch pages (another popular size for worship service guides); or six panels, 8½ by 4⅝ inches (an increasingly popular size for worship service guides).

Most church supply publishing houses now provided worship service guide paper with front-page color photos for 8½ by 5½, 8½ by 7, and 8½ by 4⅝ inch formats.

How Many Columns?

Decisions regarding typestyle, typesize, space between lines of type, line length, and page size all come together when the page is laid out and you decide how many columns will work best for good readability.

First, set your margins. On smaller pages (5½ by 8½, or 7 by 8½ inches) three-eighths inch on the left, right and top, with one-half inch on the bottom works fine. That leaves a 4¾ (or 6¼) by 7⅝ inch space for content. If you use the two-fold format on an 8½ by 14 inch sheet of paper, margins of one-quarter inch on the left and right margins, with three-eighths inch at the top and one-half inch on the bottom gives you a content space of 4⅛ by 7⅝ inches.

Be aware of two centers in every page, the actual center and the optical center. The actual center is the point where two diagonals, each drawn from corner to corner, cross. The optical center is always slightly above the actual center, which is why the bottom margin should always be wider than the top margin. If the bottom margin is the same as the top, the material on the page will look off-center and low on the page.

On larger pages (8½ by 11, or 8½ by 14 inches) a five-eighths inch margin on the left, right, and top, with a three-fourths inch margin on the bottom looks better. That leaves a 7¼ by 9⅝ (or 12⅝) inch space for content. Your reproduction equipment might help you make this decision. Some computer printers will not print in the one-half to five-eighths of an inch deep space at the bottom of the page. Using a slightly larger margin at the bottom is always more pleasing to the eye. Narrowing the margins more than the above recommendations will automatically make the page look more crowded.

Now you can plan the number of columns. The 5½ by 8½ inch page format should generally stay in one column with the exception of lists of names or short subjects which sometimes can work well in two. The 4⅜ by 8½ inch panel works only as a one-column format.

The 7 by 8½ inch page allows for more options. One column works, but the line length in anything below 12 pt. type gets a little long for good readability. Two columns are a little narrow, but read well in 10 pt. type. Another attractive possibility is to use a narrow column on the left (about 1½ inches wide) separated by a one-fourth inch wide space from a 4½ inch wide column on the right. The wider column is used for text. The narrower column is used for heads, headlines, and special notations. To help the reader delineate one story from the other, each article should be separated from the one above and below it by a minimum of two blank lines.

Illustrations for page formats and layouts appear on pages 72 to 75.

Keeping readability of line length in mind, design the larger formats (8½ by 11, or 8½ by 14) with a minimum of two columns throughout. Depending on the size of type, three columns is often better. (See appendix C, "Demonstrations in Readability," for evidence of the differences in readability and attractiveness with the different column widths on large-format publications.)

Going with the Flow in Page Layout

Once you have your format in hand, you need to fill it. No matter what the size of the format or the number of columns, the first page begins with a nameplate. The nameplate identifies your publication in

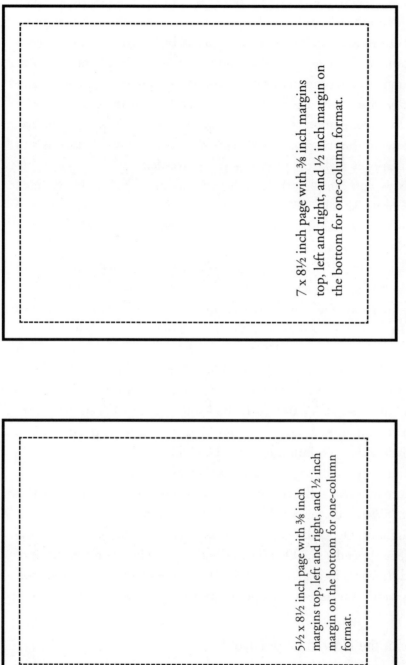

7 x 8½ inch page with ⅜ inch margins top, left and right, and ½ inch margin on the bottom for one-column format.

5½ x 8½ inch page with ⅜ inch margins top, left and right, and ½ inch margin on the bottom for one-column format.

Solid lines in diagrams mark edges of page. Broken lines mark margins for text and columns.

All diagrams are in the scale of ½ inch = 1 inch

7 x 8½ inch page with ⅜ inch margins top, left and right, and ½ inch margin on the bottom divided into a two-column format with a narrow left column to be used only for heads, headlines, and notations.

7 x 8½ inch page with ⅜ inch margins top, left and right, and ½ inch margin on the bottom divided into a two-column format.

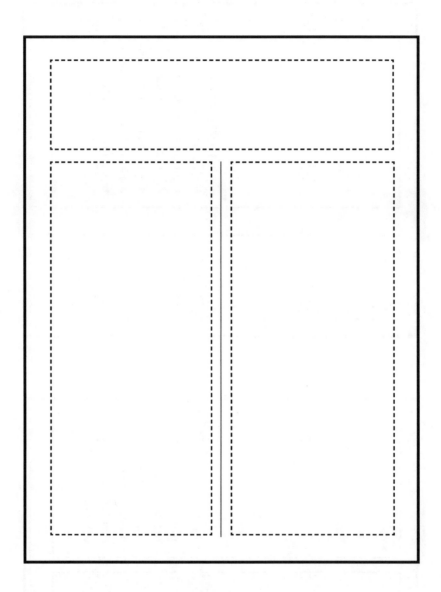

Solid lines in diagrams mark edges of page. Broken lines mark margins for text and columns.
All diagrams are in the scale of ½ inch = 1 inch

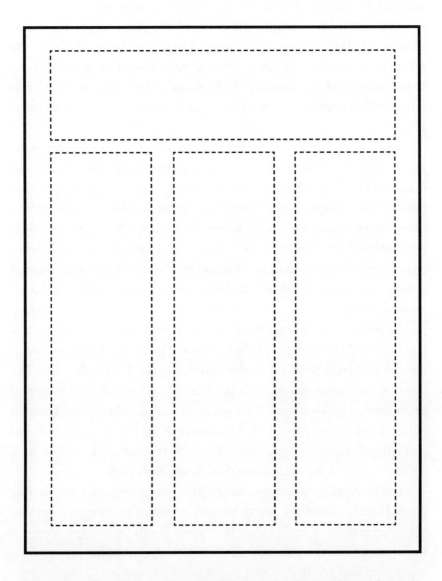

The two-column format on the left and the three-column format above work with either 8½ x 11 or an 8½ x 14 inch paper. The open block at the top is for the name plate on page 1. It can be deepened another half inch, but should not be smaller. Subsequent pages should include a line at the top for page number and identity and date of the publication. Sometimes, particularly if the type is set ragged right, a thin line between columns (as in the two-column format on the left) improves readability.

an artistic and eye-catching fashion. It usually extends across the full width of the page, and it usually is at the top of page 1.

The nameplate includes the name of the publication, the name, address, and Web address of the congregation, the date of the issue, the volume number (usually the number of years the publication has been in existence) and the number of the month of issue (with January as number 1). It should also include the congregation's logo (see chapters 12 and 13).

The name is usually in the largest type to be found anywhere in the publication. It can be an ornamental, or even a hand lettered type, but it should be compatible with the rest of the typefaces in the publication and, as always, it must be easily readable. Many congregations have shown clever creativity when they chose the name for their newsletters. Some, unfortunately, have crossed the line from clever to cute. (Information in chapter 13 regarding the development and use of a congregation's logo can also be helpful when you think about hand-lettered type.)

All of the other nameplate information probably works best in the typeface used for the bulk of the text in the publication and is used in decreasing sizes depending on the significance of the information. The name of the congregation is probably in 18, 16, or 14 pt. The rest of the information—address, Web page, date, and volume and number data—could be in 12 or 11 pt. The names of the pastor, staff, and congregational leaders, together with phone numbers and e-mail addresses, can be boxed and inserted on an inside page.

Use your imagination and creativity in designing your own nameplate. Here is one of the places where that list of exchanges suggested for your newsletter mailing list in chapter 3 can be helpful. Pick the nameplates from the exchanges that have unique qualities and intriguing design and see if they can be adapted for use at the top of your publication. But make sure you include the essential information listed in the paragraph above.

The example below displays how all the elements needed in a nameplate might work together. The entire nameplate was developed using the "Drawing" tool in Microsoft Word, one piece of clip art (from "Insert" / "Picture" / "Clip Art"), and 48 pt. Franklin Gothic Demi type for the name and Times New Roman for everything else. The dots used for separation in the address line were picked up from the Times New Roman Character Map.

Good Tidings

The monthly newsletter of **First Presbyterian Church**
6152 Olive Garden Rd. • Westminster, Ill. • (901) 123-4567
www.FirstPresb.com

September 2003   Vol. 14, No. 9

All pages subsequent to the first page (or cover) should carry a header that identifies the name of the publication, the name of the congregation, the date, and the page number. It is a good idea to separate header text from the other content of the publication with a thin decorative line and at least two lines of space.

Now you are ready to place in the content. Start on page 1 directly under the nameplate with the most important story of the month. Give it a headline that starts on the left margin of the first column to the left and runs across at least two columns. It should be in large type—one 30 or 24 pt. bold line or two 24 or 18 pt. bold lines of equal length. One blank line of space is left under the head.

The text starts under that blank line in the left column and flows to the bottom of the page. If the story is long enough, the text continues to the top of the middle column (in a three-column format) under the head, and flows down the column as far as it will go.

If the lead story ends within one and a half inches of the bottom of the page, make a slight adjustment to shorten column one and move a few lines to the top of column two to make them a bit more equal in length. A photo appropriate to the first story could be inserted at the top of column two, extending the story into the third column, or at the top of the third column.

A second story on the page could start either with a one-column, two- or three-line head in 18 or 14 pt. boldface type or a two-column head of one 18 pt. line or two 14 pt. boldfaced lines above nearly equal length columns at the bottom of the page. If you use the latter option, the text of the first story flows from about the middle of the second column to the third column where it ends just above the second story with the two-column head.

It is best not to carry the ends of stories to inside pages unless it is absolutely necessary. If you do carry part of a story inside, make sure you indicate at the bottom of the column that the story continues someplace else and give the page number. The continuation inside should be identified by a key word from the story content with a line that it is continued from the page where the story originated.

For instance, if the story is about action by the council, the inside continuation could be headed simply "Council" or "Council Actions" in 12 or 14 pt. flush left boldface heading followed in a second line by "continued from page 1" in flush right 10 pt. italic. Leave one blank line and then pick up the continuation of the story.

Your options in page layout are nearly limitless. What is most important is that you always keep your reader in mind to make sure the material can be read easily from top to bottom and from left to right without losing any part of the story.

All inside pages follow the same principles. Start with a major story on the top in the left column and let the material flow into place naturally. Since most parish newsletter stories are relatively short, try to fit the stories so that the heads form a series of triangles (middle, low, high in three successive columns) and are never right across from each other in juxtaposed columns. Review layouts in popular weekly news-magazines and corporate newsletters and adapt those ideas freely to your publications.

The last page of your newsletter also needs special attention at the point where it includes the space for mailing. First, in the upper-right corner of your mailing space (it does not have to be a whole page) you need to include a small box identifying the congregation's nonprofit third-class status, permit number, and location where the publication is being mailed. The upper-left corner must include the name and address of your congregation.

Check with your local post office regarding third-class, nonprofit status and its specific regulations. Also check with your post office regarding other mailing regulations, particularly the way in which your third-class publications must be sorted, labeled, and prepared for delivery to your post office, and the way publications must be fastened at the edges so they can be processed by automatic equipment.

The procedure of fastening your newsletter at the edge that is not folded can be a problem. Not every household has a staple remover, and if you staple the pages together at the edge, the people who receive the publication sometimes nearly destroy it to get it open—not what you want after you have spent so much time and energy in its produc-tion. A better way is to use one or two adhesive circles to tape the edges of the pages together. Check with your post office to get its recommendations and the latest information on postal regulations.

The Use and Abuse of Boxes, Call Outs, and Large Initial Letters

Boxes are a popular way to call special attention to shorter announcements or other brief pieces of information. However, they cause problems in many parish publications because the word processor's default has been set to allow almost no space between the inside edge of the box and the text. That default can, and should, be changed.

Here is how it works. Move your cursor to the list at the top of the toolbars and click on "Format." In the menu that drops down, click on "Borders and Shading." In the "Borders" box, click on "Options" (lower-right corner). You now have a menu that allows you to set the space top and bottom and left and right between the text and the inside edge of the box. A setting of 9 pts. at the top, 12 pts. at the bottom, and 9 pts. left and right works well.

In longer articles that span two or three columns, call outs can be useful and attractive typographical devices. A call out is a short phrase taken from the text that emphasizes significant content and intrigues readers enough to make them want to find out more. It can be placed to cut across the margin between two columns or be inserted across the span of one column. Usually it is set in type slightly larger than the text that surrounds it. Sometimes it is set in boldface or italic.

Some kind of device is needed to separate the call out from the main body of the text. That device can be lines (also known as "rules") at the top and bottom, a color block behind the call out (with the type either overprinted or reversed), a box or partial box. Whatever device is used, it must have space around it so that the words of the call out do not look or feel crowded. Second colors can be used effectively with call outs if that production option is available.

Another attractive typographical device is the large initial letter at the beginning of a paragraph. The size of the letter can vary depending on how big an emphasis you want and the kind of graphic impression that is appropriate.

Your word processor knows the procedure as a "drop cap." Here's how it works. Highlight the initial letter. Go to "Format" in the list at the top of your toolbar. Click on Drop Cap. You can now decide on whether you want the letter in the body of the material or offset in the margin. If the drop cap is to be in the body of the material, you need to choose how many lines it should be set in.

For most newsletters, a drop cap in two or three lines is big enough. Now you can choose the typestyle, but keep it simple. Usually, you will want to use either the same face as the text or, if you are using a different font for headlines, you might want to use that font instead. Finally, you need to select the distance you want the drop cap to be from the regular type. Play with this a bit until you are comfortable with the choice you make. This is another decision related to aesthetics.

You are probably aware by now that nearly every typographical decision you make for any publication involves a lot of decisions regarding fonts, font size, and spacing. In order not to have to make those decisions more than once, develop the practice of making notes. Once you are satisfied with the size and spacing of a drop cap, the style that sets apart a call out, the spacing around and inside of a box, make some notes that record your most pleasing decisions. The notes you make will help you not only to be consistent within each publication, but also in similar publications to come.

You might also want to note fonts and font sizes, column configurations, and other details about word usage and graphics so that you do not have to "reinvent the wheel" every time you go to work on another publication. As you lock in and record those decisions, your publications will have a consistently pleasing and readable look for all of your constituencies.

Those notes, by the way, can be made easily on your computer while you are at work on a publication. Simply click on the icon that looks like a blank sheet of paper, label that page "Publication Notes," type what you want to remember, and save the page as a separate file in your publications folder (maybe with the style sheet you are developing).

Ragged Right or Justified?

One more decision will wrap up your work on readable typography. Should the lines of text in your columns be ragged right, centered, ragged left, or justified? A flick of your fingers on one of the sets of little horizontal lines in the toolbar at the top of your screen can change any highlighted text from one to the other. (Note that when you hold your cursor on any of the four sets of lines in the toolbar, a drop-down flag identifies them, from left to right, as "Align Left," "Center," "Align Right," and "Justify.")

First, let's dispense with the options that you almost never want to use. "Center" might work for a limited number of posters and worship service guide inserts; however, it should never be used for large blocks of text.

This paragraph, set with all lines centered, makes the point.
Readers in the Western world work from a left
of the column orientation.
Anything that does not have a common left margin
forces a reader to shift
back and forth
through an uncommon left margin.
That's hard and slow reading.
Don't make your readers do it.

Readers want that common margin on the left with which they are comfortable and familiar. "Align Right" shows lines with a common right margin. That's only a half step up from centered. Check it out in the aligned right (also known as flush right) paragraph below.

Blocks of type that are set flush right (as this one is)
are almost as bad.
The flush right style might be workable
for a bit of explanatory text that
can be set up against a larger block of type
that is the major story to which it relates,
but, once again, the form
forces readers into an unfamiliar and uncomfortable
reading style that is slow and difficult.

This leaves two choices, "Align Left" (also known as flush left) or "Justified." Justified gives the publication a neat and clean pattern where both the left and right margins are always even except for paragraph indentations and the short lines (widows) at the end of paragraphs.

Those spaces, by the way, also improve readability by building in "breathing room" to keep the text from turning into oppressive-looking gray blocks, which is one of the reasons that newsletter articles should have lots of paragraphs, and no paragraph should be longer than eight to ten lines.

> Justified text defines the columns precisely. Check out this paragraph as an example. As can be seen in this sample, however, the process of justification (not a theological term in this context) sometimes forces extra large spaces between words and occasionally adds spaces between letters which are unnatural and, again, hard to read. Note the difference between the last line of this paragraph (normal spacing) and all the lines above it.

One choice, "Align Left" (the first box in the toolbar), remains. Review some contemporary publications. Many newspapers have made the transition in the last decade to align left (more popularly known as flush left or ragged right) for much of their material. Newsmagazines, self-help publications, and many other magazines on newsstands have done the same. Even sophisticated publications such as *National Geographic* and *Smithsonian* now set the text for many special features ragged right.

Many of the examples in this book are set ragged right (see, for example, pages 33, 45, 53). The only thing to be concerned about with ragged right is control of the length of blank space at the end of each line. That includes being alert to hyphenation and trying to avoid more than two hyphenated lines following each other.

But the important thing for newsletter designers and editors to know is that ragged right works. It is easily and quickly read and it is becoming more and more popular in much of the professionally edited and designed public media.

One final consideration. Ragged right also works well with ragged bottom, the practice of allowing columns of type to end at different spots on the page without filling in the blank spaces that result. A space of up to an inch at the end of one column, followed by a column that fills to the bottom of the page, followed by a third column that ends an inch and a half from the bottom, is aesthetically pleasing.

By all means, avoid filling those spaces in with clever sayings, Bible verses, or clip art. Never forget: blank is beautiful. The blank spots (white spaces) that are allowed to remain on a page often set that typography apart as the most aesthetic, the most pleasing, and the most readable.

The process of choosing typography and designing format stretches an editor's creative imagination in the production of an attractive parish publication that appears to be vital, important, and interesting. But if the editor has too short a list of potential content, researches the potential stories poorly, or writes the material badly, no amount of sophisticated typography will hold on to the reader for long.

The key to readership is substantive content written to inform, educate, and motivate all of the appropriate audiences. That's next.

6

Content Ideas and Organization

All examples cited are actual notices and articles found in bulletins and newsletters over the past two decades. Names and places have been changed. The rewrites often include material added from the author's imagination in order to provide enough information to complete the story as it should have originally been written. Note that each rewrite is only one of several possible ways that the original story might be improved.

No matter how clear and concise the writing, no matter how readable the format, none of that matters if the content is not the substantive information that reflects a congregation's life and ministry.

In order for an editor of a parish's publications to be certain everything of significance is included in each issue of the periodic newsletter, the worship service folder, or a publication connected with a special event, she must start building the table of contents well in advance. Otherwise, significant announcements might be inadvertently left out, valuable space might go unused or be used poorly, and the congregation will be depending upon constituencies that are uninformed or much less well informed than they should be.

Once again, your word processor comes to your rescue. Everyone on the staff—from editor to pastor to part-time office assistant—should have two easily accessed networked computer files. One file is named "Bulletin Content Ideas" and the other is named "Newsletter Content Ideas." Now, whenever anyone thinks of any idea for content that might be appropriate in either publication, that person writes it down in the appropriate file in her computer. Those who do not have computers at their workstations should have their ideas added to the files of any staff member who does.

Note that the responsibility for the generation of content ideas does not rest exclusively with staff personnel. The president of the congregation and the chairs of congregational committees should always be encouraged to suggest ideas they and the groups they lead might have for articles or concerns that need attention in writing.

Everyone in your church office can make this procedure even easier by creating short-cut icons for the content ideas files they have opened in Word. Simply find the file in "My Documents" (Windows 98). Using a right click on your mouse, drag the icon of the file to your open screen. A short menu will appear offering: "Move Here," "Copy Here," or "Create Shortcut Here." Click on "Create Shortcut." Then, a single left click of your mouse on that short-cut icon will bring your content ideas file to the screen immediately.

Developing Newsletter Content Idea Files

Now that you have the files, what do you put in them? Start with the file you named "Newsletter Content Ideas." Some general subject categories should be standard. You might even want to establish a system with subcategory folders within the subject categories. Individualize the list for your congregation.

Church council meeting announcements/reports
    (see chapter 4 regarding printing of minutes)

Standing Committee meeting announcements/reports
- Worship and Music
    List of scripture texts for the coming month
    List of sermon themes/outlines for the coming month
    Prayer list of parishioners who are sick, hospitalized,
        homebound, grief-stricken
- Education programs
    Adult forums
    Teen forums
    Children's classes
    Catechetical instruction
    Bible study groups
    Adult membership preparation
    Opportunities in the community for continuing education

- Evangelism
    Introduction of new members
    Listing of transfers to other congregations
- Stewardship
    Report of congregation's giving record by month/year to date
    Relationship of giving record to approved annual budget
    Special benevolence opportunities
- Building and grounds maintenance

Special Committee meeting announcements/reports
    Building committee
    Anniversary celebration committee

Announcements of meetings and programs for auxiliary organiza-
    tions (see chapter 4 regarding the use of organization reporters)
    Women's groups
    Men's groups
    Youth groups
    Ushers
    Altar guild
    Prayer groups

Personality features (individuals and their families)
    Members of the council
    Chairs of standing and special committees
    The organist, choir directors, and other musicians who assist in
        worship on a regular basis
    New members
    Lists of members in college and the military with notes of interest
        gleaned from letters and conversations with members of the
        family

Education regarding the faith group at large
    Mission fields and missionaries supported by the congregation
    Colleges supported by the congregation
    Seminaries supported by the congregation
    Bible camps and retreat facilities the congregation supports and
        uses
    Personality profiles of leaders in local, regional, district, and
        national judicatories

References and recommendations for reading regarding articles in the national church magazine that could inform, educate, and inspire the members

Letters and editorials from staff or volunteer leaders
What theme would best serve the people of the congregation now?
Who is the best person to write about that theme? (It doesn't always have to be one of the pastors.)

Photos
What stories might include photo coverage?
What person or event should be the focus of the photo(s)?
Who takes the photos or where can they be obtained?

Production timetable
(perhaps you will want this at the top of your list)
Date of staff meeting to discuss publication, its contents, its production, any foreseeable editorial problems
Deadline for all stories and photos to be submitted to editor
Deadline for publication to be ready for printer/copier
Deadline for mailing

As you are putting your newsletter together, you might also want to develop a brief table of contents that will alert readers to the most significant stories. Such a list could fit on the first page, or near the mailing space on the back page.

The above outline obviously does not fit the periodic newsletter of all congregations. The list needs to be tailored to each congregation's potential and need; however, do not abbreviate it lightly. Consider the possibilities it offers for a lively, creative, professional, printed communication that will be anticipated and welcomed by members of all the congregation's audiences and compete favorably with other media calling for their attention.

If you are wondering where you might find the information and educational material regarding the national and international faith group, check the Web site for your denomination. It is full of more material than you will be able to use in a year. Remember, too, that information on the national and international ministry can be repeated at least once a year, updating the material as denominational Web pages or other sources might indicate.

Using Your Newsletter to Plow the Ground of Stewardship

Furthermore, members of a congregation who are provided with educational material about their national faith group and its worldwide ministries every month do not require a crash course each fall when it is time for the annual stewardship drive.

When every issue of the newsletter includes denominational information, then—when the annual stewardship drive time comes around—members only need to be reminded of where their benevolence dollars go and what they accomplish. As members receive regular updates about world missions, the establishment of new congregations in the United States, the services and programs available from social-service agencies, and educational opportunities in colleges and seminaries, their responses to the need for both prayer and finances for those ministries becomes a daily concern rather than only a seasonal emphases. Such a stream of information builds an entirely different base from which to ask for support. The annual stewardship campaign can then be more of an emphatic reminder of what members have already been told—assuming that the newsletter climbed over the competition and was read and digested soon after it arrived in each parishioner's mail.

Pruning the Ideas to Fit Your Congregation's Resources

Perhaps the above list overwhelms you, and you are perplexed by the fact that the congregation in which you work has not provided either enough people or a big enough budget to produce a monthly newsletter as large as all of the ideas suggest. Instead, choose what you can do well, give priority to those things that are most important, and fill every paragraph with objective substance that reflects the ministry and life of the congregation and its people in helpful and interesting language and design.

Over recent decades, I have reviewed many parish newsletters that use as much or more space as the above outline suggests might be needed. Unfortunately, few of those publications had the substantive, objective content the above outline helps to provide. With their paucity of substance, these publications would have been vastly improved if they had used less space while providing more significant information.

Some things, such as a listing of sermon themes a month in advance, might be impossible in the congregation where you serve. Having been a parish pastor with the pressure of weekly sermon preparation, I understand the problem; however, some pastors are able to make this happen and I applaud them. They have an advantage over colleagues who cannot.

The above planning tool has several advantages for content management. It's easy to keep on your word processor, it's easy to amend and erase when a particular content idea has been completed, and it's easy to carry good ideas that did not fit in the last issue forward to the next. A lot of good ideas for content—in fact, some of the best ideas—are not critically time-sensitive. They will still be good ideas three, six, or nine months later when time becomes available to develop them and space is available to get them into print.

Writing Stories Early

Perhaps the biggest advantage such a master newsletter content file provides is the one that is most subtle. Check the list on your computer every couple of days. If the office computers are networked so that you can check the files with content ideas from other staff, check those as well. If the computers in your office are not networked, ask for a printed copy of the lists being generated by other members of the staff once a week. Some things on the lists—information about worship services, actions of the council, reports for committees—will usually be rather straightforward. Most of the information is already at hand, and a phone call or two will fill in any information that is still needed.

Although many people do not like to admit it, everyone in every office always has occasional open spots in the workload. The time to make more creative use of the open spots is the "early warning" time toward the beginning of the month when you see an item about which you are already fully informed on the content list. Take the 10 minutes of open time to write the item then and file it in your word processor for use when the newsletter is put together toward the end of the month. If another member of the staff generated the content idea, it is probably most efficient to have that person write the story since he is likely to be most conversant with the information.

Whoever writes the item, that person should write it in the typeface, line length, and line spacing that is standard for your newsletter format. Then, when the editor is ready to assemble the newsletter, the space needed for the article is obvious and it can be fit more quickly into the publication's format. In Microsoft Word, check out the "Auto-format" function in the "Format" file on your word processor toolbar. Set it up to be used when appropriate. Then the finished story can simply be copied from the "early writing" file and pasted into the appropriate place in the newsletter as it is being put together. The editor writes and places the headline as the story is positioned in the newsletter.

Note that it is best to "copy" rather than "cut" the story when moving it from the file to "paste" it into the publication format. Then it is still available in case it accidentally disappears in transition. Finally, make sure the item is crossed out (not deleted, but marked with a line through it) on the master newsletter content file and a date has been put behind it indicating when it was written. Now everyone knows that story is ready, and others on the staff know they need not worry about it anymore. Delete the item from your list only after the newsletter has been published and you have started the new master content list for the next month.

Now look at how you might develop your "Bulletin Content Ideas" file.

Developing Bulletin Content Idea Files

Because of the nature of the bulletin (a service guide for all worshipers), some content is standard every week. Use the list below as a starting point. Fill in details appropriate for the congregation where you serve.

Identifying Information
    Church identification
    Church address (Note: You know who and where you are, but prospects and visitors might not be so sure, particularly after they get home.)
    Phone number of the church office and home phone number of at least one pastor
    Hours when the church office is open during the week
    The date (Here is one place where use of the year is not only appropriate but needed for record and archival purposes.)

The liturgical designation for the day of worship (Christmas, Easter, the tenth Sunday after Pentecost, the third Sunday in Lent, etc.)

The clergy staff

The lay staff

The organist, participating choirs, and their directors

Members of the congregation helping as readers, cantors, assisting ministers, greeters, ushers

Artist or designer of the bulletin cover

Introduction to the service

General theme of the appointed scripture texts for the day

Key to identification of hymnals and service guides being used in this day's worship

Music notes regarding the composers and writers of anthems and hymns

Notes on the liturgical season and its significance

Notes on the liturgical paraments and vestments

Welcome to worshipers

(Review chapter 7 to remind yourself of the difficulties with subjective language that so easily creeps into the welcomes in bulletins of too many congregations.)

Guide to the order of service

Order of worship (useful whether the service is formal or informal)

Sermon theme and text

Sermon outline

Hymns

Anthems or other special music

Acknowledgments and notes of gratitude

For donors of flowers and other decorations in the chancel and sanctuary

Memorials

Announcements

Prayer list of parishioners who are sick, hospitalized, homebound

Reminders of major events taking place in the coming week (supports newsletter stories)

Reminders of next week's forum topics and other special opportunities for education

Reminders of sign-up procedures and deadlines for special programs

Special benevolence needs and procedures to participate in them

Financial report indicating amount received at last week's worship and whether that is behind or ahead of the amount needed by this date according to the approved annual budget

Brief updates on recent progress or problems

Schedule for the week to come
Opportunities for education
Meetings of official boards and committees
Meetings of auxiliary organizations
Music groups rehearsals
Social functions
Next week's worship schedule

Making the Most of Content Possibilities

Special occasions such as building programs, seasonal worship series or education programs, and anniversaries overflow with opportunities for congregations to expand their vision and generate interest in communities beyond their membership (the neighborhood, the larger town or city, other faith groups). Yet too many congregations, apparently frightened of being thought of as being overly aggressive, either ignore such opportunities completely or use them badly. Consider the following example as reported in an article that appeared some years ago in the newsletter of a congregation in Michigan.

BUILDING NEWS

The decision of the Special Congregational Meeting on Sunday, July 31st was "lets get going!" With that vote of confidence the responsible officers of the congregation will be signing the contract with the contractor and arranging for interim financing during the construction phase.

The deadline for the signing of the contract is September 7th. We will probably be signing it around the end of August so that construction can

```
begin the first part of September. With good luck
during the rainy Winter months we could be ready to
use the new addition by Christmas.
```

```
                    BUILDING FINANCE
```

```
  The final contract for construction came to just
over $192,000. In order to get it that low we have
agreed to eliminate some of the items that we can
do later on. We will also be doing much of the fin-
ish work and painting ourselves.
  In addition to this we will need your committed
financial support. Those who have made pledges to
our Building Program are requested to review them
and keep them up to date. If you haven't yet made
your pledge do so today!  Pledge cards are avail-
able in the church office. Place your card in the
offering or you can give it directly to Pastor or
Xxxx Xxxxxxxx. We are $16,000 short of cash and
pledges to complete the project. We believe in you
and your ability to respond to that need. Let us
join hands and go forward together to the glory of
God.
```

The article nearly filled one 7 by 8½ inch page. The remaining space at the bottom of the article was used for one piece of clip art consisting of communion symbols and the words, "Given and Shed for You."

Let's consider a few of the questions a reader might have asked when first confronted with this article, as well as questions the writer or editor should have asked before putting it into print.

In paragraph one of "Building News":

- What is the name of the congregation?
- Who are "the responsible officers"?
- Who is the contractor?
- What is being built? What is the building going to look like?
- Why isn't an architect's drawing or floor plan included?
- Why aren't groundbreaking and datestone laying services announced?
- Why aren't the "Building News" and "Building Finance" headings developed into more active, interesting, and fact-filled headlines?

In paragraph two of "Building News":

- Could the date for the beginning of construction be more specific?
- Who are the "we," and are the second "we" the same as the first?

In paragraph one of "Building Finance":

- Who are the first "we" who "have agreed to eliminate some of the items . . ."?
- Who are the second "we" who "will also be doing much of the finish work and painting ourselves" (and do they know it)?

In paragraph two of "Building Finance":

- Who are the "we" who "are $16,000 short"?
- Who are the "we" who "believe in you and . . ."?
- Why doesn't someone thank members of the congregation for already having pledged 92 percent of the needed funds?

A rewrite of the original story follows. Note that it starts with a headline rather than a heading, and the headline is a summary of the substantive material that follows.

Also note that much information, including names and identities, has been added to answer the questions listed above. That information, not available when the article was rewritten, was filled in with fictionalized "facts," the kind of information that should have been included in the first place. Also note that both the responsibilities and authority have been passed around to the lay leadership of the congregation and are not the pastor's exclusive purview.

Construction to Begin on Education Unit With Groundbreaking Service on Sept. 3

Christ Lutheran Church will celebrate the beginning of construction on its new education unit with a special groundbreaking service at 9:30 a.m. between worship services on Sunday, Sept. 3.

Every child in the congregation is invited to bring a small shovel to participate in the special ceremony, according to Philip Johnson, director of parish education.

Stephanie Erickson, building committee chair, said, "The long-awaited addition became a reality during the special congregational meeting on July 31 when the congregation voted overwhelmingly to get started with the project."

Construction contracts will be signed this week by Elmo Nordquist, congregation president, and William Hoffman, treasurer, according to Pastor James Luther.

The general contractor with the low bid was Steeple Construction Co., headed by Dwight Redburn, a long-time member of the congregation.

The contract was negotiated down to slightly more than $192,000 when the church council agreed that it would be able to find volunteer workers in the congregation to help with interior finishing and painting.

Weather permitting, construction will begin on Monday, Sept. 4, the day after the groundbreaking. The contractor expects to have construction finished in time for Christmas.

Pastor Luther was enthusiastic in his praise of the members of Christ Lutheran for their support of the project. He said, "Although a small amount of interim financing might be necessary, pledges and cash now available for the project already add up to almost 92 percent of the total needed."

"Such response is an indication of excellent stewardship," Pastor Luther said. "I encourage any members who have not yet become a part of this project to make their pledges soon. Only $16,000 more is needed."

Pledge cards are available in the church office.

The new, one-story addition will be attached to the east end of the present church structure and extend to the south to form an "L." The red brick exterior will match the present edifice.

The 4,000-square-foot unit will include six classrooms, a large lounge with a small kitchen, space for a library, and new offices for the pastor and church staff. The present office spaces will be converted into classrooms as part of the construction project.

President Nordquist said, "Christ Lutheran has been working toward this addition for a long time. It will increase substantially the congregation's ministry in education while also making it possible for groups in the community to use the facilities for meetings and other activities.

> Additional celebrations connected with construction of Christ Lutheran's new education unit include:
> - Datestone laying ceremony—Oct. 1
> - Dedication ceremony—Dec. 31

(A line drawing of the floor plan for the addition is included at the end of the story in place of the communion clip art.)

Note the differences between the original story and the rewrite.

Readers of the rewrite know the name of the church and the nature of the construction project as soon as they have read the first sentence. They also know the names of all of those previously unnamed "responsible officers." The story has been filled with the names of every layperson who has had anything to do with leading this project to its current status. Furthermore, all of those "we's" have been identified.

Also note the details of the groundbreaking announcement. In most small- to medium-size TV markets, having a horde of children breaking ground with their plastic sandbox shovels is going to draw video coverage that will be aired on the news that evening. If that does not happen, at least one photographer from the local newspaper is going to show up. If neither of those things happen (or even if they do), make sure a member of the congregation with a good camera and some experience in how to use it creatively takes photos of the occasion for the congregation's own newsletter and archives. (See chapter 10 for more on photography.)

If the congregation does not have a member who has the equipment and capability to be that photographer, hire a professional or make arrangements with the newspaper photographer to buy a photo or two (these people always have many more photos than the paper will use). Once that groundbreaking service is over, consider it over. It cannot be rescheduled a month later for the photo that the congregation wishes it would have had the foresight to plan in the first place.

Using Newsletter Ideas to Generate News Releases for Public Media

Note that the form of the story rewritten for the newsletter also will serve as a news release for public media. Assuming good relationships have been cultivated in advance with all media, that release should be sent to specific editors or reporters no less than one week in advance (preferably 10 days). Accompany the release with a line drawing of the floor plan and a copy of the architect's drawing of the addition. See chapter 9 for more details on dealing with the mass media.

Follow up the mailing of the news release and other materials with a phone call or personal visit a couple of days later. The second contact confirms that the news release was received, answers any questions that the editor or reporter might have, and tries to learn how much of a commitment to covering the story the paper and the stations are willing to make. The person making the second contact will also have a list of phone numbers at hand in case the editor or reporter wants to contact any of the people mentioned in the release for further comment.

When the paper and stations indicate that they plan on covering the groundbreaking, the contact person makes sure someone meets those representatives of the press (reporters, photographers, video crews) when they arrive at the building site. The contact person welcomes the media representatives, helps them find their way around, gives them a copy of the printed groundbreaking program, introduces them to congregational leadership, and helps them to find (and reserve) the best vantage points to cover the story.

Some might question whether the news release should include the funding information regarding the $16,000 still needed, the call for those who have not pledged to do so now, or the availability of pledge cards. If the media thinks this is inappropriate material—and most media in larger markets will—they will cut it. If, on the other hand, the media thinks it is appropriate to report this part of the story in their communications vehicle—and some media in small towns will—the congregation has a chance to spread its base of support.

It is not uncommon for a congregation that announces its needs publicly to receive substantial gifts from members of the community who are nonmembers. When people of means are impressed by a congregation's growth and ministry and see it as an asset for the whole community, they sometimes decide to help the congregation themselves by writing sizable checks in support of its program.

A congregation that is afraid to pursue that possibility aggressively will never know if such largess from unexpected sources might also substantially enhance the finances for its ministry.

More about Stewardship

One other stewardship question must be discussed. Look again at the last paragraph of the original newsletter story.

```
In addition to this we will need your committed
financial support. Those who have made pledges to
our Building Program are requested to review them
and keep them up to date. If you haven't yet made
your pledge do so today!  Pledge cards are available
in the church office. Place your card in the offer-
ing or you can give it directly to Pastor or Xxxx
Xxxxxxxx. We are $16,000 short of cash and pledges
to complete the project. We believe in you and your
ability to respond to that need. Let us join hands
and go forward together to the glory of God.
```

Consider the situation. The total building project is going to cost $192,000. The congregation has already received $176,000—92 percent of the total. Only $16,000 is needed to meet the goal, and they still have yet to break ground or begin construction. Most congregations would be overjoyed with such a response.

But where do you see any joy in this paragraph? Where is the thank you to people who have already made their pledge? Your parish publications can affirm that stewardship is about more than asking—it's about being appreciative of the efforts of the people who respond, and letting them know of that appreciation as well. Stewardship is about the celebration of gifts given out of love as people respond to a need. It is not about berating members for amounts not yet received.

Note the difference in the response of the pastor in the rewrite.

Pastor Luther was enthusiastic in his praise of the members of Christ Lutheran for their support of the project. He said, "Although a small amount of interim financing might be necessary, pledges and cash now available for the project already add up to almost 92 percent of the total needed."

"Such response is an indication of excellent stewardship," Pastor Luther said. "I encourage any members who have not yet become a part of this project to make their pledges soon. Only $16,000 more is needed."

Should effusive praise be necessary when members of a congregation do what they are expected to do anyway? Probably not. But how much easier is it going to be to have a satisfactory response the next time the congregation has a fund drive if the people know that their previous efforts in stewardship have been appreciated? And how much more excitement and enthusiasm for their congregation and its mission will they pass on when they meet friends and neighbors who might be looking for a church home?

Satisfied parishioners, thanked parishioners, excited parishioners are better stewards and better evangelists than those who wonder even a little bit whether their gifts, their time, and their faithfulness are appreciated.

True, faithful members do not do what they do for words of appreciation. They do what they do because it is God's love in their lives that motivates their faith and their response. They know that it is God's glory, not their own, that is what is essentially important. But published evidence of appreciation from the leadership of the congregation does not hurt.

Making the Most of the Time

Building projects are among the most expansive in generating congregational celebrations—do not let them go by unnoticed. Think about the special occasions that a building project similar to the one under discussion could generate in your congregation.

First, of course, is the groundbreaking service. If it can be done by children with sandbox shovels, everyone's going to have a great time, and the participating children might begin to feel more a part of the congregation than ever before. If you are going to try this procedure, make sure the ground where the ceremony is to take place is spaded up in advance and the soil is loose. Then the children will actually be able to do some "ground breaking" on their own with their plastic shovels. Another hint: make sure a handful of extra sand shovels are available for the children who forgot theirs. That way, every participant will have a lot more fun.

Second, consider a ceremony for the laying of a datestone. Is it just a solid stone with the date inscribed? Or might it be a hollow dated stone that would hold a box with materials that make it into a time capsule? If it's a time capsule, the congregation can have a great deal of fun collecting appropriate materials that will reflect the time for people who might open it with great expectancy 50 or 100 years from now.

The datestone for an education building would certainly include a printed program for the datestone ceremony, the previous month's newsletter, and that Sunday's worship service folder. It might also hold a photo (black and white) from the groundbreaking and a current newspaper (the one with the groundbreaking story and photo would be good). Since the building is oriented to education, it might also include curricula materials, a pencil, a small box of crayons, a small container of white glue, the printed program from the children's most recent Christmas program, and a group picture of all the children in Sunday school classes.

Celebrating the dedication of the new building is next, but perhaps a week or two earlier the congregation would like to have a special service celebrating the service of the Sunday school teachers. Not only would the current teachers be honored, together with the director of parish education, but maybe former teachers who have moved away could be invited back as special guests. Of course, this kind of celebration also calls for food, whether it's coffee, milk and cookies, a catered lunch, or a potluck dinner.

Plan for the dedication to include all the members who had leadership roles in the building. It should include having at least one ribbon-cutting ceremony with oversized ribbons and oversized scissors. It might include having a key to the main door passed from the contractor to the architect to the parish education committee chair to the pastor to the parish education director to a teacher representing all of the other Sunday school staff.

All of this, of course, would be interspersed with appropriate prayers, liturgical responses, and benedictions led by the pastor and other worship leaders. Hymns and choir anthems (especially by children's choirs) might also be a part of the celebration.

The point is, whenever your congregation has any kind of opportunity for special celebrations, make the most of them in the most creative ways possible with well-publicized celebratory programs and appropriate publications that people will hold on to as keepsakes. Don't miss any possibilities. These events don't come around that often in the lives of most congregations. Creativity engenders excitement, satisfaction, enthusiasm, and, most of all, joy. Try it and see what happens.

The Archival Imperative

Note in the style sheet in appendix B that years should not be designated when writing current dates in the context of an article or report unless it is necessary to avoid confusion.

However, historical and archival considerations necessitate several exceptions. The year must be designated in conjunction with the date of publication of periodic newsletters, worship service folders, and printed programs for special events. Think what happens a few generations later if the year is left out in the identifying information for such publications. People who come after you to write the congregation's history, research the past for some form of historical notation, or put together a book celebrating a specific anniversary will not be happy with your less-than-complete communications efforts.

Designation of the year need not be in the announcement of a regular monthly meeting. However, it is extremely important that the year be included on the cover or in the nameplate or masthead of publications for special events to verify archival authenticity for future generations.

To clarify, the nameplate is the identification of a newsletter usually found at the top of page 1. It includes the name of the publication, the name and address of the congregation, the date of the issue, the volume number (usually the number of years the publication has been in existence), and the number of the month of issue (with January as number 1).

The masthead is usually boxed and printed on page 2, 3, or 4. It includes the name of the publication and the names (with phone numbers and e-mail addresses) of the editor and writers. It might also include the names of the pastoral and lay staff and the congregation's officers. The name, address, phone number, Web page, and e-mail address of the congregation should be included. Newsletter production information, such as the monthly deadline information for articles and the date the publication is mailed, also are usually included in the masthead.

Making the Communications System Work

Now let's analyze a congregation's communications opportunity to see how it works. Within recent decades, many congregations with traditions of midweek services during the season of Lent began to expand that ministry beyond worship to include a soup and bread supper before the service.

When the congregation in which I am a member began the practice of pre–midweek service suppers years ago, I thought the primary purpose would be to provide a simple meal inexpensively for families who would come to eat and stay for worship. I soon noticed that quite a few people came to the supper a half-hour or more early and waited till the people in the kitchen were ready to serve. I also noticed that most of those people were elderly, and many of them were not members of the congregation.

Then came a moment of enlightenment. These people did not come necessarily because they were hungry. They came because they were lonely.

The soup and bread suppers were seen by some as an opportunity to be with other people, to converse with them, to broaden their circle of acquaintances. It was a special kind—a needed kind—of ministry that went far beyond convenient food and worship. The soup and bread suppers were a community service.

That made the suppers much more than an exclusively congregational activity. They needed to be publicized with that larger ministry in mind, which is what led to news releases similar to the one below. The sample, by the way, also provides a workable form for the preparation of news releases for newspapers, radio stations, and TV broadcasters.

NEWS RELEASE

Feb. 24, 2003
For Immediate Release

Peace Lutheran Church
1234 Winnebago Ave.
Germantown, Mich.

Prepared by: James Newton
      742-5763
      jnewton@aol.com

Peace Lutheran Serving
Soup and Bread Suppers
Before Lenten Worship

Soup and bread suppers will precede all Wednesday evening Lenten services at Peace Lutheran Church in Germantown this spring.

The suppers will be served by members of a different organization or group in the congregation prior to worship services each week beginning on Ash Wednesday, March 5.

"The meals and worship will be times of nourishment, refreshment and fellowship for all the members of the congregation together with other members of the community," said the Rev. William Hurstpa, pastor of Peace Lutheran.

The suppers will be served from 6:00 to 6:45 p.m. in the Peace Lutheran fellowship hall. The 45-minute worship services will begin at 7:00 p.m. in the sanctuary.

People who are not members of Peace are invited to attend the suppers and are encouraged to stay for the worship services afterwards. Cost of the suppers will be a $3.00 donation for adults and $1.50 for children ten years old and under.

Pastor Hurstpa said he was excited about the new and non-traditional prelude to the traditional week-day services of worship leading up to Holy Week, Good Friday and Easter.

He said, "Lent is one of the most important liturgical seasons for Christians as they contemplate the sufferings and death of Jesus in his redemptive work for all people. The suppers add a dimension of community for those who are lonely and seek company in this significant season."

Ash Wednesday worship on March 5 will include the service of Holy Communion. Pastor Hurstpa will introduce the general theme for the weekday services, "Standing at the Foot of the Cross."

The soup and bread supper on Ash Wednesday will be prepared and served by members of the church council. Other organizations in Peace Lutheran serving the suppers during the Lenten season are the senior choir, the youth group, the executive committee of the Women of the Church, members of the board of parish education, and the young singles club.

Peace Lutheran is located at 1234 Winnebago Ave. in Germantown.

Extending the Use of the News Release

Do not stop working on this story once the news release is finished. Now that it is in hand, use it as the foundation for newsletter articles and bulletin announcements written in advance and filed for use at the appropriate time. It will take less time to write the whole package if you do as much of it as possible the first time you work with the material and all the information is fresh in your mind.

First, copy the news release to another word processing file. Now, working with that material, format and edit it to fit the style of two stories for the March issue of the parish newsletter. That work will result in two newsletter stories that might look something like the following.

Lenten Services Preceded by Suppers at Peace This Year

The traditional mid-week Lenten services will be preceded by non-traditional soup and bread suppers at Peace Lutheran Church this year.

The combination of food, fellowship and worship will begin on Ash Wednesday, March 5, and continue for five more Wednesday evenings prior to Holy Week.

The suppers, each of which will be prepared and served by a different group or organization at Peace, will begin at 6:00 p.m. and continue until 6:45 p.m. in Fellowship Hall. Worship services will begin at 7:00 p.m. in the sanctuary.

Those attending the suppers may contribute a $3.00 donation per adult and $1.50 per child ten years old and under to cover costs.

The first supper on Ash Wednesday will be prepared and served by members of the church council. The supper on March 12 will be served by members of the senior choir; March 19, the youth group; March 26, the executive committee of the Women of the Church; April 2, members of the board of parish education; and April 9, the young singles club.

No supper will be served in connection with any of the worship services during Holy Week.

Note that the above story covers details of the soup and bread suppers, but does not give any information about the worship services. Now you need to expand on paragraph eight in the news release to give members of the congregation a more complete picture of the thematic treatment they can expect in their midweek worship. That second story might look like this:

"Standing at Foot of Cross" Theme for Lenten Meditations

The general theme for the mid-week meditations at Peace Lutheran to be preached by Pastor Bill Hurstpa during Lent this year will be

"Standing at the Foot of the Cross." All will be based on the story of Christ's passion in chapters 22 and 23 of the Gospel of Luke.

The first, during the service of Holy Communion on Ash Wednesday, March 5, will be "Standing at the Foot of the Cross: Receiving His Body and Blood."

Other meditation themes will be: "A Test for Greatness" (March 12); "A Time for Prayer" (March 19); "The Power of Darkness" (March 26); "Nothing Deserving Death" (April 2); and "Who Is the Innocent?" (April 9).

The schedule for services during Holy Week and Easter will be announced in the April issue of the Peace newsletter.

It's probable that the Lenten series articles will be the lead stories in the newsletter. The pastor's letter (which will be included farther back in the publication) is the perfect place to emphasize the congregation's Lenten plans with a focus on the history of the holy season rich in tradition and what it should mean to the members of Peace Lutheran Church.

Now you have a news release for the public media and two stories for the March issue of the monthly newsletter finished and saved in your files. One communications mode remains—announcements for Sunday worship service guides.

Copy the newsletter announcements to another file, and format and edit the announcements that you will use for at least the first two Sunday worship service guides. The first would appear on Sunday, March 2. It might look something like this:

A Soup and Bread Supper

will initiate the Lenten season at Peace as a prelude to the midweek Ash Wednesday worship service on March 5. The supper, being prepared and served by members of the church council, will begin at 6:00 p.m. The service of Holy Communion will begin at 7:00.

Now, while you're on a roll, write the bulletin announcement for Sunday, March 9. If you anticipate success, it could read:

More People than Expected

attended the soup and bread supper and stayed for Ash Wednesday worship services last week. The combination of food, fellowship and worship is expected to be popular again for the mid-week service on March 12. Theme for the second in the series of meditations on "Standing at the Foot of the Cross" being preached by Pastor Hurstpa is "A Test for Greatness." The supper begins at 6:00 p.m.; the worship service starts at 7:00.

Obviously, if the turnout for the soup and bread supper was smaller than anticipated, the announcement has to be changed to reflect what really happened. Save the worship service guide announcements in a standing "Bulletin Contents" file, and you are ready to move on to another communications challenge.

The planning and organization of the information you put in your parish publications is critical to their substance and readability. Without such planning, important material can be forgotten, significant opportunities for education might be overlooked, and articles and announcements are written in such a rush that they end up as incomplete and ill-defined shadows of the real story.

Furthermore, the congregation's total communications program feels fragmented rather than coordinated and well thought out. Planning pays, but it takes discipline to put it in place and use it effectively.

Now it's time to give more attention to your weekly worship service guide.

7

Worship Service Guides

Potential bulletin content was discussed in the last chapter, but worship service guides, commonly called bulletins, have their own set of writing and production problems. Now is the time to address those problems. Your style sheet discussed in chapter 4 still applies. Concerns for readability discussed in chapters 4 and 5 are the same and call for the same kinds of answers in the choice of fonts, typesize, and line length.

You know from the analysis of audiences in chapter 3 that only 30 to 35 percent of the congregation will see your congregation's bulletin on most worship days. You also know that space is limited more severely and announcements are primarily reminders of events and programs that already have been given fuller treatment in the periodic newsletter.

Three of the four purposes—to inform, to educate, to motivate—are the same. But the fourth purpose in that list, to edify, moves nearer to the top and takes on a more important meaning. Bulletin content is dominated by the guide to the order for worship. That guide is intended, more than anything else, to help members and visitors alike to have an edifying and uplifting experience for that hour they are in corporate worship each week.

Take Stock of the Covers

Start your review of your congregation's worship service guides by studying the sources of your bulletin covers. Should current practices be continued or modified? Does the congregation purchase a bulletin cover service that provides full-color cover pages (photographs or other art)? Does the editor, other office staff or a lay member produce bulletin covers with the use of clip art from word processing programs or other services? Does the congregation have enough artists and graphic designers among its members so that bulletin covers are created free by these talented members on a weekly basis? Do you use a standard bulletin cover featuring a full-color photo, a watercolor painting, or a line drawing of the church building? Depending on the talent available in the congregation and the willingness of those gifted members to participate, all of the above options are viable.

If a cover service is purchased, does it include meditative text regarding the season or the prescribed texts for the worship day on the back cover? If that is the case, the space available for material specifically related to your congregation's worship and weekly program is limited to the two inside pages unless you prepare and include a series of inserts. Inserts will be revisited toward the end of this chapter in the section, "Dealing with the Question of Inserts."

Getting the Identifying Information Right

Too many congregations shortchange themselves by downplaying the identifying information. The leadership in those congregations reason, "When people come to worship here they already know where they are. Why use space proclaiming the name, address, staff, and phone numbers related to this congregation?" The reasons go back to the principle that you never assume that anyone knows anything about the subject or situation other than yourself.

Consider the possibility that a family has just moved into town and their house is only three blocks from your place of worship. In fact, one of the reasons they bought that house was because of its proximity to a place of worship. They decide to visit on a Sunday, and when they enter your sanctuary and sit down for worship, they want and need to know something about the congregation and its ministry. And the first place they find that information is in the content of the bulletin that identifies the name of the congregation and its staff. If, when they get home, they have questions, it will be easier for them to get in touch with people who have the answers if those people's phone numbers are readily available.

The identifying information should also include the date (with the year for archival reference) and the liturgical name of the day of worship.

All of this information need not be static. The editor should sit down on a slow day and keyboard all the information (in no particular order) that might be included. Make the name of the congregation slightly bigger and bolder. Drop supporting information into blocks of smaller type that are flush left and flush right. Perhaps you can add a small version of the congregation's logo. Then move all the elements around on your word processing screen until you have an attractive and logical arrangement of the necessary facts.

When you are satisfied with a format for this information, highlight the whole block and file it as an AutoText entry. AutoText is a shortcut that allows you to save and insert frequently used text and graphics, and can be found in the "Insert" menu at the top of your toolbar. While the identity block is highlighted, click "new," and then decide which category you want to put it in and what you want to call it. In order to provide some variety, do the whole exercise again, rearranging the data in a different format. Put that one in another AutoText file and now you can alternate headings every Sunday or on different liturgical seasons.

In large congregations with many people on the staff, the list of personnel can be inserted at the end of the bulletin—but it should be somewhere in the publication. You might also want to add the names of the chair and members of the council. Never forget that bulletins are all about helpfulness.

Writing the Welcome

One of two pieces of information needs to come next: either a word of welcome, or instructions that will help people find their way through the worship aids in the pew racks. Let's deal first with the welcome. Writers of the "Welcome" included in most worship service guides are too often sucked into the trap of subjective language, as if it were quicksand. Consider:

> **WELCOME TO ALL!** May we bask in the sunshine of God's presence as we worship. Let us reach out in Christian love to as many other worshipers as possible. Blessings! **If you are a visitor**, we invite you to sign our guest book, listing your name and address. **Gathering as God's Family**, we invite baptized believers to come forward to Holy Communion. Young children may come forward for a pastoral blessing.

The example is afflicted with more than one problem. First, the "Welcome" might strike some people in the pew as a bit "over the top" in its colorful enthusiasm. Second, it's redundant. Third, it uses undefined we, us, and our language (see Dealing with Those Pesky Pronouns on pages 47-50 in chapter 4). Fourth, the use of boldface twice in the middle of the text seems to be arbitrary and without purpose. Fifth, the subject of the announcement moves rather brusquely from a welcome to communion participation instructions.

Here's one way to solve some of the problems. The rewrite tones down some of the effusive enthusiasm, gets rid of the redundancy, avoids difficulties with the subjective third person personal pronouns, softens the separation of members and visitors, and uses boldface only once at the beginning of the welcome.

> **Welcome to all who worship at First Methodist this morning.**
> May members and visitors together bless each other in the joy of God's presence. Visitors are encouraged to sign the guest book at the entrance to the sanctuary. Everyone who is baptized is invited to come forward to Holy Communion and bring young children to receive a pastoral blessing.

The problem with inclusion of communion participation information would be solved better if this material were inserted in the order of service where the communion liturgy is introduced.

One more thing. Note that the lead sentence has been changed to boldface only. In the original example, three means of emphasis—boldface, all caps, and underlined—were used at the same time. Such multiple uses of emphasis add up to graphic overkill and are completely unnecessary.

Also note that the first words of the welcome are boldface, cap and lowercase, and the remaining material uses a hanging indent with all lines indented a couple of spaces below the boldface first sentence. The hanging indent is a good graphic devise to isolate one bulletin announcement from another while using a minimum of space.

To set a hanging indent on your word processor using Microsoft Word, click on "Format" in the toolbar, then click on "Paragraph." Click on the "Special" box in "Paragraph," scroll down with the arrowhead on the right and highlight "Hanging." Now move to the "By" box, which allows you to change the indent designation (which is probably defaulted to ".5"). Change the "By" designation to ".2."

The writing of welcomes also produces other traps. Consider the following:

> **WELCOME TO FAITH LUTHERAN CHURCH.** We all come to our Lord Jesus Christ, but the door through which we enter to eternal life is narrow. Entry into the Lord's kingdom is a gift to those believers who live faithfully in accordance with the teachings of Jesus Christ. It is not easy to enter through the narrow door. It takes commitment to the Lord!

If I were visiting a congregation, sat down in the pew and read that "Welcome," I might be tempted to find a more welcoming place to worship. Here is what probably happened. The pastor was writing the welcomes and tailoring them to relate to the content of the Gospel for the day. But this one, a challenging text from Matthew 7, led the writer to use language that reflects mostly law and not very much good news. It is useful to read what you write and consider both its purpose and its affect before you put it into print.

Try this alternative:

> **Welcome in the Name of Our Lord Jesus Christ to** worship at Faith Lutheran Church. The Gospel for this day (Matt. 7:13-14), part of Jesus' Sermon on the Mount, reminds us all that discipleship can be difficult, but also helps us to see the forgiving love and grace of God. Please sign the guest book in the narthex as you leave.

Notice the difference in both tone and temperature. The original comes across as insensitive and cold as ice. The alternative includes the toughness of the Bible passage, but retains a welcoming warmth.

Guiding the Worshiper through the Service

Bulletins are about helpfulness. In many denominations, a virtual library of hymnals and other books of worship confront visitors when they sit down in the pews. Even members are confused. The most useful bulletin clarifies the purposes of these books and makes clear which ones are going to be used in the day's worship.

I have worshiped in congregations where three different aids to worship were in the pew racks, and no instructions were given

111

regarding which ones were going to be used at what times during the service. Members familiar with the worship practices of the congregation did not seem to be having any difficulty in participating. I, on the other hand, was lost. It was not a pleasant feeling and not as worshipful an hour as I had hoped it would be.

Some Lutheran congregations solve the problem by including an introductory notation similar to the one below:

Helps for following the order for worship

Page numbers are at the bottom of the page in the front section of the worship book. Hymn numbers are at the top of the page in the hymn section of the book. The color preceding the reference in the order of service indicates which book to use: green for *Lutheran Book of Worship;* maroon for *Hymnal Supplement;* blue for *With One Voice.* An asterisk (*) invites worshipers to stand.

The notation regarding the asterisk raises a question. Why is an asterisk used if the pastor or other worship leader consistently gives a hand signal that directs the congregation to either stand or sit? I have worshiped in congregations where the appropriate posture was signaled for each element of the service even when the asterisk had already provided the instruction.

If the worship leader failed to give the hand signal called for in the bulletin, however, the congregation seemed to be at a loss to know what to do. Sometimes about a third of the people followed the instructions of the asterisk while another third waited for the confirming hand signal. The remaining third was caught somewhere in the middle, an awkward posture at best. Perhaps it would be better to go back to the older and more traditional practice of using hand signals only and omit the asterisk.

Another helpful practice is to include a succinct sentence that ties together the appointed biblical lessons for the liturgical day in one unifying theme. Such information can be incorporated in the bulletin either right after the introduction of the date and liturgical designation for the day or as a separate announcement towards the top of the announcement page.

Formatting the Guide to the Order of Worship

Liturgical churches sometimes have a formatting problem when they simply list all of the elements of the worship service in order. It is a lot of information, and without some form of organizational or graphic embellishment, such a list is aesthetically dull, graphically monotonous, and hard to follow. Solve those problems by organizing the worship guide into named sections that help worshipers through the service. Then, as the worshipers are being guided, they are also being taught basic elements of worship.

The following examples of service organization might be helpful.

Gathering (up to the Bible readings)
Word (Bible readings through the sharing of the peace)
Meal (offering through post-communion prayer)
Sending (benediction and dismissal)

We Gather to Worship (through prayer of the day)
We Gather to Hear God's Word (Bible readings through sermon)
We Respond to God's Word (prayers through offertory prayer)
The Communion Liturgy (kind of an add on to the organizational pattern)

Opening the Service (prelude through hymn following Kyrie)
Hearing God's Word (Bible readings through hymn following sermon)
Responding to God's Word (sharing of the peace through offertory)
Celebrating Holy Communion (communion liturgy)
Closing the Service (prayers through closing hymn)

We Confess Our Sins (invocation through prayer of the day)
We Hear God's Word (Bible readings through sermon)
We Respond in Faith (sermon hymn through offertory prayer)
The Great Thanksgiving (communion through closing hymn)

Gather Joyfully (prelude through prayer of the day)
Grow Spiritually (Bible readings through service of communion)
Go Faithfully (blessing, closing hymn, postlude)

The Preparation (hymn of invocation, invocation, confession, absolution)
The Entrance Rite (introit through the collect for the day)
The Liturgy of the Word (Bible readings through the prayer of the church)

The Liturgy of the Eucharist (offering through communion)
The Post-Communion (post-communion canticle through
closing hymn)

Use the headings boldface in caps and lowercase, flush left or centered. Use one size larger type than the rest of the text (for example: 12 pt. heading with 11 pt. text) and insert a full line of space above each section notation. Note that while these organizational devices work best for liturgical worship, they can also be useful for forms or worship that are less formal.

It is a good idea to include the sermon text and theme at the point where the sermon (or homily) is designated in the order of worship. Some worship leaders also include an abbreviated version of the sermon outline to help people in the pew follow development of the theme and exegesis of the text more easily.

Music notes can also be useful. Who is the composer of the tune, who is the author of the text, and what are their nationalities? When did they live and when was the composition written? Did a particular event stimulate creation of the music? If the text being sung is not in English, can a translation be provided?

Liturgical churches follow a specific calendar of seasons. Include details of the liturgical season, something about its traditions, the significance of the colors of the paraments and vestments and the meaning of the symbols they incorporate. Check the Web pages of your judicatory offices if such information is not available in your pastor's study or the congregation's library.

One other notation might be helpful in the order of worship. Some faith groups do not use extended corporate silent prayer except on special occasions (such as midweek Lenten services). When people in the pew are not familiar with the use of silent prayer in public worship and are not called upon to participate in it frequently, the feeling of being uncomfortable with the practice is almost palpable up and down the pews.

Consider including some silent prayer "starters"—a few words that would help people frame petitions and fill this private time more productively. Perhaps a brief scripture text, a few verses of a psalm, or an appropriate hymn verse would be helpful as stimulation for the worshipers' silent prayers and meditations.

How Much of the Service Needs to Be Printed?

Another question needs consideration. Should the entire service—including hymn texts, the words to prayers, creeds and scripture texts—be written out so that the worship service is complete in the worship service guide? Or should worshipers be directed to the page numbers of hymns and the elements of liturgy printed in the hymnals and other books of worship available in the pew racks? Many congregations also have Bibles in their pew racks, or encourage worshipers to bring their own Bibles to the sanctuary with them.

It is easier for worshipers to follow the entire service with all the texts complete in one printed guide. So what is the down side?

First, it is considerably more work and takes many more pages and much more production time to include all the texts of all the elements of worship. But another factor might be even more important long term. Most hymnals and other books of worship include considerably more than several different liturgical settings and a large collection of hymns that might be sung throughout the year. They also include occasional services for baptism, reception into membership, marriage, and funerals as well as a vast collection of prayers that are not used corporately on a regular basis.

If the service guide includes all the language of every element of worship, how does the average parishioner become acquainted with the meditative treasures that are part of their religious history? The congregation makes a large financial investment in hymnals and other worship helps. Members of the congregation, as well as prospective members and visitors, can learn from those resources and become acquainted with the traditions that mold the week-by-week practices of personal piety and public worship.

Printing every detail of every worship service in a too-comprehensive worship guide does not encourage people in the pew to investigate, discover, and use the broader tools of meditation and personal piety at their disposal.

Don't Forget Copyright Credits

One more important consideration. Copyright law insists that notices of permission to use hymn texts and music must be included in the publication in which that material is printed. That permission must be obtained by contacting the publisher of the book in which the material appears.

Most publishers of hymns and liturgical texts give such permission free of charge. Some, however, have usage fees large enough (often, several hundred dollars) to make you want to choose another hymn.

If you want to print the text and music of a hymn or portion of liturgy in your worship service bulletin, you must plan far enough in advance to get the publisher's permission and credit that publisher in print. The publisher will provide you with the appropriate language for the printed notification. Some music and texts are in the public domain and can be reprinted without copyright notation. The publisher will notify you of such circumstances when appropriate.

Choosing and Writing Bulletin Announcements

At last we have come to those ubiquitous weekly announcements. Let's start with acknowledgments and notes of gratitude. Usually, the list will be limited to memorials and those who provided flowers for the service. If you have already included greeters and ushers in the list of personnel, it is not necessary to give them a special word of thanks. Remember, space in the bulletin is at a premium, and efficient use of that space is essential.

Check out the duplication in the five items below, included as they originally appeared (with all names changed to protect privacy).

> **Altar Flowers** are given to the glory of God and in loving memory of my grandmother, Amelia Oelston, by James Johnson.

> **We are saddened** by the death of Jane Corbatt. May the joy of the Resurrected Christ comfort her family and friends in their time of need.

> **The Service** this morning will be dedicated to the memory of Jane Corbatt.

Altar Flowers are given to the glory of God and in loving memory of Jane Corbatt by her friends at First Baptist.

Altar Flowers are given to the glory of God and in loving memory of Madeleine Hardy and Kent Javinsky by the Hardy and Polsdad families.

That's a lot of space with an overload of duplication and a crowd of clichés to talk about deaths, memorials, and altar flowers. Try this as an alternative:

The worship service this morning
is dedicated to the memory of Jane Corbatt, a long-time member of First Baptist Church, who died quietly at her home on Feb. 10. She was 97. The yellow roses on the altar were given by friends in her memory.

Other altar flowers are given
by James Johnson in memory of his grandmother, Amelia Oelston; and by the Hardy and Polsdad families in memory of Madeleine Hardy and Kent Javinsky.

By removing the flower basket clip art, the space used has been cut from 19 lines (plus the art) to 12 lines.

Now we can deal with the regular announcements. Even though you might have accumulated a long list of potential content (see chapter 6), most subjects will fall within four categories:

1. The prayer list for members who are grieving, sick, or homebound
2. Reminders of the more significant events and meetings that have already been announced in detail in the current month's newsletter
3. Brief reports of progress on recent problems or concerns
4. The skeletal schedule of opportunities for ministry, worship, and education for the coming week

Formatting Announcements

The formatting of announcements is just as important as the formatting of newsletters. If you crowd all the announcements together on an 8½ by 5½ inch page, they look tiresome, and many of them will neither be read nor remembered.

First, allow at least a half a line of space, and preferably one line, to separate each announcement. Leave that space blank. You defeat the purpose of the space if you fill it with a centered row (short or long) of crosses (plus signs), stars, or other ornaments. Work for readability, not decoration, and never forget, "Blank is beautiful."

One way to give each announcement the attention it deserves is to start the sentence with the subject and use that introductory language in boldface, cap and lowercase over one-fourth to three-fourths of the length of the first line. Then simply continue the item with a standardized hanging indent without boldface under the boldface lead in.

See the examples above in the rewrites of welcomes and acknowledgments for flowers and check the section on "Writing the Welcome" earlier in this chapter for instructions on setting up hanging indents on your word processor.

Dealing with the Question of Inserts

The busy life of contemporary congregations and the full schedule of opportunities for ministry make it increasingly difficult to get every announcement that seems to be needed into the space left over after the order of worship. That fact brings us to the question, "How many inserts are enough?" And that question always leads to a more realistic, "How many inserts are too many?"

Make no mistake: inserts are a problem. When members sit down in the pew before worship with bulletin in hand, what do those people do to prepare for the service? First, they remove the inserts. If they have come 10 to 15 minutes early, they might have time to read them then and put them in their pocket or purse to take home. Or, if they make an early, and maybe premature, judgment that the content of an insert does not appeal or apply to them, they simply leave it in the hymn rack or on the pew.

If they come into the sanctuary a few seconds before the service begins, they have to try to shuffle the bulletin and all its inserts while holding the hymnal and Bible (or two different hymnals) needed for participation in worship. That can be disastrous, and the paper blizzard that flutters to the sanctuary floor is both embarrassing and disruptive.

None of that engenders the kind of meditative preparation for worship that the congregation tries to encourage and participants would like to experience. Furthermore, the communication process those inserts engender is at best flawed and at worst counterproductive. How can a congregation avoid such a mishmash of less than worshipful responses?

Some alternatives are possible.

One, do not allow any inserts to float free. Fasten them into a single, bound package of 8, 12, or even 16 pages by collating the bulletin into numbered pages fastened at the fold with a saddle-stitch stapler.

Two, instruct ushers to hand out the inserts to every family as they leave the sanctuary following the service.

Neither of those options is particularly satisfactory or practical.

The best alternative is to cover all of the material that fills those somewhat extraneous pages with detailed articles in the periodic newsletter. Then, if reminders seem to be necessary, make those reminders in brief one- or two-sentence announcements in the bulletin, referring them to the additional details in the newsletter that every member has already received at home. The bonus for this method is that everyone in the congregation receives this information, not just the 30 percent of the membership who happens to have attended worship services on that Sunday.

It takes tight writing to boil a 10-paragraph newsletter story into a two-sentence bulletin reminder. But it can be done when you use all the appropriate abbreviations, avoid every adjective and adverb, and stay brutally objective. Even with the best of brevity, however, on some days of worship all the needed announcements simply will not fit in the available space without resorting to inserts.

Occasionally, every bulletin editor has to deal with some standard exceptions. If your congregation purchases a service whereby all of the scripture texts, the appointed psalm, and the prayers for the day are printed on both sides of a 5½ by 8½ inch page, then there is an insert that you want to use. The same is true of small, poster-like inserts that are sent out by regional or national judicatory offices, although it would be better to include them within the pages of the newsletter.

If you do not want to clutter the newsletter with inserts either, than reproduce or rewrite the information for inclusion in that publication's standard format. It is more work, but it might be more effective because it gives the reader a more consistent style of writing and design and packages the material as an integral part of the other important announcements.

Choosing and Using the Appropriate Format

If your congregation buys a bulletin cover service, you usually have three format choices. They are:

1. 8½ by 11 inch paper with one fold to make four 8½ by 5½ inch pages;
2. 8½ by 14 inch paper with one fold to make four 8½ by 7 inch pages;
3. 8½ by 14 inch paper with two folds to make six 8½ by 4⅝ inch panels.

If your congregation prints its own bulletins, you have a little more flexibility, but not much. The finished size of the bulletin is still determined pretty much by the size of the sheet of paper you start with unless you want to, as professional printers say, "cut to waste." Bulletins for special services can use 8½ by 11 inch paper vertically to produce a four-page 11 by 4¼ inch publication.

After the paper has been selected and you know the page size, determine the margins. The same principles apply to bulletins as were recommended for newsletters in chapter 5 (see pages 69-71). Margins that work best for all of the page sizes listed above are ⅜ inch on the top, left, and right, and ½ inch on the bottom.

The size of type should not be dropped below 10 pt. If the demographic profile of your congregation shows that more than a quarter of the congregation is aged 65 and older, those people will be much more comfortable with a type size of 11 or 12 pt. As with newsletters, serif typefaces are the most easily read.

Both the 8½ by 5½ inch and the 8½ by 4⅝ inch page formats should be restricted to one column that would be 4¾ inches or 3⅞ inches wide. The 8½ by 7 inch page, however, can work with two 2¾ inch columns separated by ⅜ inch space. A popular use of the 8½ by

7 inch format is to set up the order of worship in six-inch-wide columns and deal with all the announcements in two columns. Most important is to make sure the recommendations regarding readability in newsletters are applied with the same regularity to the design of bulletins.

The Problems with Oral Announcements

A word is needed about oral announcements. I have visited worship services where I have been handed a bulletin full of informative and motivational announcements; however, the pastor takes time during the service to reiterate every one of them. When a congregation gets locked in this pattern, members have a tendency not to read the announcements printed in the bulletin because they know they will be reminded of them orally anyway. It's best to avoid the duality.

At other worship services I have visited, the pastor asks, "Does anyone have any announcements?" Members start standing up to announce the meeting of the women of church auxiliary that week, or the need for more people to clean up after the potluck dinner next Wednesday night, or the shortage of drivers and chaperones for the youth outing that afternoon. Sometimes such announcement time seems interminable, particularly for visitors.

The problems with such practice are fourfold. First, it interrupts the mood and substance of the service of worship. Second, only a relatively small part of the congregation hears the announcements. Third, the congregation has no written record of any of these needs and concerns for later publicity. Finally, any details that are announced only orally are absent from archival records.

In addition, a visitor can get the idea that this congregation definitely does not have its act together when it comes to effective promotion and public relations affecting its ministry. It should be both your goal and your mission to do everything possible to make sure such a negative response happens as infrequently as possible.

The next chapter deals with issues of responsibility and concurrent authority to deal with those kinds of concerns and difficulties.

8

Issues of Responsibility and Authority

Many people in congregations have responsibilities. The pastor is responsible to conduct worship services and preach sermons (among many other things). The organist is responsible to play the organ (and maybe the piano) for worship and sometimes carries the additional responsibilities of choir director. If a congregation has a separate choir director, that person is responsible to choose anthems and help select hymns to be sung during worship. The janitor is responsible to unlock and lock the church, mop and shine the floors, dust the pews, mow the lawn, shovel the walk, change the light bulbs.

All those responsibilities—and many more—need to be done. In addition to responsibilities, some of those same people also have authority. The pastor is called to be the spiritual leader of the congregation. The organist chooses music appropriate to the season. The choir director selects the music for anthems and rehearses and conducts the choir. The janitor buys the necessary supplies for cleaning and maintenance.

The secretary is responsible to be the receptionist, answer the telephone, sort the mail, keep the files current, type and mail letters, and—oh, yes—produce a weekly worship service guide and a monthly parish newsletter and a few other special publications. In some congregations, the responsibility for producing parish publications is handed over to a paid or volunteer editor so that the secretary can avoid going into weekly overload.

Sadly, far too few leaders in far too few congregations also give their secretaries or editors appropriate authority to write, edit, design, and distribute parish publications as well as the responsibility to produce them. The secretary-editor often has training and experience in writing clearly and concisely, using the word processor effectively to design readable layout, and making decisions regarding the most significant, interesting, and appropriate content.

However, when such persons try to use their training and experience bolstered by fresh ideas that will improve the congregation's communication ministry, they find to their chagrin that they have not been given the authority to change the outdated communications practices of past decades.

Pastors and members of councils sometimes claim, "We've never done it that way before," and insist on maintaining the status quo, bad as the status quo might be. Or, some publications editors are told to leave a badly written article in its original, uncommunicative form, rather than improve it with needed rewriting and additional facts in order not to hurt the feelings and dent the ego of the original writer.

In the production of parish publications and the development of congregational public relations, the conferring of authority goes hand in hand with the assignment of responsibility. That mandatory duality helps to foster a healthy working relationship within the total office staff (including the pastor) as well as ensuring a better quality of published communication for the whole congregation.

Learning from a Case History

Within a week of a half-day workshop I conducted on parish publications, I received e-mails from two of the participants. Their unfortunate experiences provide detailed case histories regarding the consequences of editors who have responsibility without authority.

The first e-mail arrived the day after my workshop. The congregation's secretary, who also doubled as the person responsible for the production of the bulletins and newsletter, had come back to her office to be confronted by an irate member, angry because the secretary had the audacity to edit an article the member had written for the newsletter.

The article literally cried for changing. The original, exactly as written and submitted (including the multiple typographical errors) except for changes in names and identities, read:

**TO HAVE OR NOT TO HAVE THE FAIR BOOTH
AT WA CTY FAIR THIS YEAR
THAT IS THE QUESTION!!!**
Anyone interested in anyway to help with planning, working,setting up,
cleaning etc. please come to planning meeting on MAY 5th between services
in fellowship area. This is a way almost every member can participate in
shareing the message of Jesus Christ to many who have never heard or felt
His love through another person. In the last 3 years we have had members
pray for the booth,give money for cookies and toys for childrens game,set up
booth, take down booth, sew costumes,pick up ice,pick up cookies in Harvest Falls and bring to fair,work at booth,visit booth,send others to
booth,some have filled water coolers,worn costume,donate Christian items
to give away, place stickers on guests of our booth and again many praying
for us at the booth.(someone forgot to pray for cool weather last year, I think)
See you on May 5th.!!!!!

Mabel Mistable 785-321-1234

The secretary who served as editor knew—as just about anyone with
an objective viewpoint would—that this piece needed a lot of work.
She rewrote it as follows:

Washington County Fair

Christ Lutheran Church offers an exciting opportunity for its members to minister to the people of our community by serving on the
committee to coordinate the booth at the Washington County Fair.
There will be a meeting on Sunday, May 5, at 9:25, to discuss the
many ways that you can help: working on booth preparation, costumes, games for the children, errand runner or spending a shift at the
fair. No amount of time is too small—we need many hands and
hearts for this important event. Comments from years past have been
very positive and supportive. If you would like to help, but cannot
attend the meeting, please call Mabel Mistable at 321-1234.

The evangelism team is also asking that if you have Bibles and
devotional materials in good condition that you are able to donate,
please place them in the box in the fellowship hall. They will be
given away at the County Fair.

That's a considerable improvement. Unfortunately, "Ms. Mistable"
was not convinced. Even worse, the pastor sided with the parishioner
and told the secretary, "Well, maybe you should write it the way she
told you to." That's responsibility without authority. That's sad.

A Letter to Ms. Mistable

In my response to the secretary, I included a letter addressed to Ms. Mistable that could be forwarded to her. It said, in part:

> Church communication, even at the parish level, must be the most professional communication possible because it is in competition with every other form of communication received and considered by every potential reader. Leaders of a congregation can never assume that people will read their publications simply because they are members of that church.
>
> One of the most important audiences that receive a parish newsletter are those people who are least active and seem least interested in the mission and program of the congregation with which they should be associated. Good parish communication might renew their interest.
>
> Let's look at your original article. The headline you offer is far too long and does not offer the reader much substance regarding the specific content of the article to follow. Professional reporters and essay writers seldom write their own headlines. The editor has to write the headline because only she knows where the article will be placed and how much room is available. Furthermore, 46 exclamation marks do not give any more emphasis to a statement than one. The English language does not recognize 46 exclamation marks as a legitimate form of punctuation. One is all that is called for. . . .
>
> The heading also includes an unusual abbreviation, WA CTY. That's a potential problem for the reader who is not as conversant as you with this subject. Never assume that anyone knows anything about what you are writing except yourself. Then you will automatically take care to make sure that everything you say is complete and well defined. . . .
>
> The first sentence should include the "who," "what," "when," "where," and "why or how" of the subject of the announcement. When I put your heading and the first sentence together, I still don't have enough information about what this article is about. Most of the other readers of this material will have the same puzzlement. When that happens, too many readers simply move on to something else because nothing substantive has grabbed

their interest. Also, when is the fair this year? It would help prospective workers to know when they would be needed. . . .

Finally, some substantive facts about last year's fair booth would help prospective booth workers be more motivated to offer their services. How many people visited Christ Lutheran's booth last year? How many dozen cookies were given away? How many toys were given to children? How many gallons of water did visitors drink? Did visitors to the booth who were not members of Christ Lutheran comment on the booth? What did they say? How long has Christ Lutheran been sponsoring the booth at the fair?

I hope you know that your efforts on behalf of Christ Lutheran Church, its evangelism committee, and the fair booth project are invaluable contributions to the life and ministry of the congregation. The information you provided to the editor for inclusion in the newsletter is extremely important both to her and to the congregation. However, with her responsibility as editor, she needs to have the freedom and authority to edit and rewrite material to make the Christ Lutheran newsletter the most effective communication it can be to all who read it. I learned as a writer that sometimes I was too close to the material to reflect it properly in my writing. The editor could stand back from that writing, see its weaknesses, and alter it to improve its impact.

On the next page you will find one way I would rewrite your original story if I were editor of the Christ Lutheran newsletter. I hope the rewrite is useful. Note that I've made up some information in order to fill what I see as blanks spots in the original material your story offers.

One More Rewrite

The editor's rewrite had been a big improvement. However, it still had some blank spots in the information, and those blank spots needed to be filled. Here's the alternative I suggested:

First Planning Meeting May 5 for Booth at Washington County Fair

Members of Christ Lutheran Church interested in serving on the planning committee for this year's booth at the Washington County

Fair will meet at 9:25 a.m. between worship services on Sunday, May 5.

The booth, sponsored by Christ Lutheran as a special ministry, has been a popular stopping place for visitors to the fair for the past three years. Last year, 3,678 people registered as they stopped in to enjoy a cookie, a cool drink of water, or a toy for their child.

The 2002 fair will be held on Aug. 1–4.

Several visitors testified how much they enjoyed the quiet respite from the usual fair noise and excitement when they stopped by for some refreshment and conversation last year.

The planning meeting on May 5 will begin the organization of volunteers who will be available to set up and take down the booth, sew costumes, pick up ice and cookies, fill water coolers, and be available during the fair to greet visitors.

Mabel Mistable, fair committee convener and coordinator, said, "The Washington County Fair has become an important part of Christ Lutheran's summer ministry. Lots of volunteers are needed, as well as members who will donate gifts, support the fair project financially, and pray that the booth be an effective witness to the Christian faith. Members can participate in the fair booth by sharing the message of Jesus Christ with many who have never heard or felt his love before."

The fair booth is a project of the congregation's evangelism committee. Anyone in the congregation who has Bibles and devotional materials in good condition that can be used as gifts for booth visitors is asked to place them in the box in fellowship hall.

For more information, or to volunteer your services, call Mistable at 321-1234.

The Secretary's Response

When I checked with the secretary six months later to see how the situation might have improved, she wrote:

We have a "head in the sand" philosophy around here, and that's what happened to this issue.

I had a meeting with the president of the congregation and the former president of the congregation, and their basic response was, "Why not let them write as they wish and give them a by-line? That way you are not responsible for how it is written."

I pointed out that that buck stops here and I know that it is badly written and therefore is my responsibility. We ended up with them saying they would discuss it and get back to me and of course they never have. . . . There was no support from the pastor who has now left the congregation.

The interim pastor seems to be very supportive and would probably back me up on any future differences. But in the meantime, this one has just been forgotten. I get the sense that their idea of support is to just listen, pat me on the back, and move on. . . .

I feel very strongly about the newsletter and will continue to strive for the best that I can.

One of the most tragic things about this episode is that people who would never allow mediocrity in the communications department of their own business fail to see the consequences of mediocrity in the communications program of their own congregation. Overriding satisfaction with the status quo is particularly deadly in a day when retention of congregational membership is at best tentative and at worst disastrous.

Given such a perilous attitude, stewardship stumbles and evangelism evaporates. And when those vital signs of a congregation stagnate, death—or at the very least, uselessness and irrelevance—cannot be far behind. So much for case history number 1.

Another Case History

The second case history deals with a different problem, but with similar responses. Another workshop participant, this time an administrative assistant, sent me an e-mail later in the same week that I had conducted the workshop. She wrote:

I am seeking editorial control over content. The church council decided that I ought to run very long stories in the weekly bulletin if that's what the writer wants. I am in the process of assembling a "how to utilize publicity" packet for each committee chair and staff person. The packet will include:
- a very simple style sheet
- guidelines and examples of what is appropriate for each type of communication
- specific deadlines for each publication

- information on how to prepare (or how I will assist in preparing) stories for submission to local media

What I am requesting from you . . . is some "expert opinion" that I am moving our congregation in the direction of making our communications more effective. (Frankly, I don't see why the council would vote to pay for my workshop attendance and then not willingly act upon the information I obtained from the workshop!) This is a very small congregation so I am not at this time seeking to implement a "publicity committee." Also, I am only 20 hours a week and would not be able to be in attendance at committee meetings.

I have begun the process of educating our staff about publicity using the handouts you provided at the workshop . . . but somehow the idea that the bulletin and newsletter ought to be "different" because they reach different audiences in different settings . . . simply is not getting across.

Do you have a succinctly written teaching piece on the purposes of these two forms of communication? Do you have a piece on why the person responsible for these publications should not be hog-tied by the council?

That e-mail delineated the problems, but also outlined good positive steps the administrative assistant was taking to improve the situation. She also reported steps she had taken to place the story in the community newspaper as well as a monthly Lutheran newspaper of the Twin Cities called the *MetroLutheran*. That was a good move, but her efforts with the community newspaper received a lukewarm noncommittal response.

Good Story, Wrong Publication

The story that created the original fuss had been submitted by the congregation's youth director with the insistence that it be printed in the church bulletin. The council, in an unfortunate act of micromanagement, agreed with the writer. The bulletin, with its small space and relatively small audience, is without a doubt the wrong place for this story.

The original text of the story follows. Once again, the names of people in the story have been changed.

Last Sunday Gethsemane's youth group divided into teams and left church with one paper clip per team. Their goal was to visit the neighborhood, introducing themselves as members of Gethsemane's Youth Group and seeing what they could trade for their paper clip.

Mark Mohr, Jacob Spicer, Bill Wombat and David Gunderson write:

"We learned that people are sometimes reluctant to trade down. People like expensive possessions and don't like giving things when they get something worse. People like little kids but not teenagers. We started with a paper clip. We got a pencil, then a candle, then a ceramic cat, then 2 chocolate coins, then a nutty bar, then a dollar, then paper, then three bags of potpourri. That's how it ended with three bags of potpourri, paper and a ceramic cat."

David Olson, Keith Planer, Cindy Casson and Mike Fosstrom write:

"The start of the game is basically where you start out with a paper clip. Then you go door to door asking 'do you have anything bigger or better.' The first thing we got was a pen. For that we got a piece of notebook paper. For that piece of notebook paper we got an envelope. Then a very nice man gave us $2. The next lady wouldn't take the $2 and gave us some candy. Then we got some noodles for the candy. Then we got a ceramic cart. We then gave the ceramic cart to a lady from church and it was her birthday. We still had the $2. The next house we went to gave us canned goods, but wouldn't take the $2. The next house gave us two boxes of Hamburger Helper but again wouldn't take the money. We ended up with $2, two boxes of Hamburger Helper and canned goods. We learned that most people tried to help and some couldn't."

All food was put in the food drive and the money was put into the offering.

The administrative assistant explained to the writer that the piece was too long for the Sunday bulletin, and that she had sent the story to the local paper and to the *MetroLutheran*. Because the story had missed the deadline for the congregation's monthly newsletter, it would be held until the next month's issue.

A Call for Authority

I responded to the administrative assistant with a two-page letter that said, in part:

> Your most obvious problem is the connection between responsibility and authority. In congregations where a secretary or other member of the staff is assigned to produce parish publications, that person has the responsibility to write, edit and design that important part of the church's ministry. That's not enough, however. The person assigned the responsibility for parish publication production must also have the authority to make decisions regarding content, style, priorities, format and design.
>
> That does not mean that the editor should ride roughshod over every differing opinion. It does mean that doors of communication are open between the editor and the pastor, church council, writers and reporters. Differences about the handling of materials can be openly discussed and all viewpoints aired in an effort to make the congregation's publications and public relations program the best that it can be for the benefit of the whole congregation.
>
> But after all the discussion, it is the editor who has both the responsibility and the authority to make the decisions, and she deserves and needs the backing of the pastor, the council, and anyone else in the congregation who is concerned.
>
> Responsibility without authority makes the person producing the parish communication materials little more than a mechanic. It strips that person of the confidence and motivation to help make those communications the attractive, creative, useful, effective tools they should be to enhance the evangelism, stewardship, and education programs of the whole congregation. Those communications tools are a major resource in reaching out to the inactive members on the church rolls and drawing them back to more active participation in the life of the congregation. They also are the primary means of keeping in touch with prospective members and making them excited about joining a vibrant congregation. . . .

All of that is connected to the problem that the congregation's leadership—both pastor and council—seems never to have paid attention to the importance of audience analysis as it relates to the parish publication program (and, for that matter, to other programs of the congregation). Consequently, they have never thought through the relationship of bulletin to newsletter and the fact that only 30 to 35 percent of the congregation usually sees the worship service guide, while 100 percent of the congregation has the possibility of seeing the newsletter.

Thus, they have not faced the fact that Sunday morning bulletin announcements can and should be little more than reminders of the information in larger stories already published in the monthly newsletter. . . .

I am impressed by what you did with the story from the youth director. It's a good story. Contacting the *MetroLutheran* and the local newspaper was a good idea. The response you received from the newspaper, by the way, is a fairly standard way for editors to handle this kind of material. Don't be intimidated by it and follow up with a slightly changed version within the next few days.

You were absolutely right in saying that such a story does not belong in the bulletin, but needs the fuller coverage that inclusion in the newsletter would give it. In my opinion, that's not even debatable.

Finally, it's too bad the church council has so little to do that its members spend their time messing around with the micromanagement of the editor of the bulletin and newsletter. That's sad. I am also distressed that the pastor does not support you in your editorial decisions. I guess that brings us full circle to the place where I began this response.

Getting Past the "Who's in Charge of What" Question

It is difficult for some parish publication editors to get past the "I'm the only one in charge" management style of some pastors, and it is not hard to pick those people out when reading publications from their parishes. The attitudes of such pastors reflect their personal insecurity, and the ministry of the congregations they serve is often less effective than it could be. It is not easy to deal with the insecure, overbearing, only-my-way pastor. To put the shoe on the other foot, editors need to be aware that it is not easy to deal with them, either, if they are also overbearing.

The other difficult problem reflected in the first case history is dealing with the nonwriting writers who have somehow come to think that every jot and tittle they ever put down on paper is the only way something can be written. With those people, and they are legion, the editor must always be the educator, suggesting and teaching that even congregational publications call for the highest qualities of professionalism if they are to meet the competition and speak most persuasively to all of the audiences the faith group needs to reach.

One procedure introduced in chapter 4 in the section titled "Empowering the Subjective Voice" works most of the time when an editor is faced with a particularly bad piece of reporting. That is for the editor to rewrite the item and turn the reporter into an "expert witness." Here is how that might be done.

Call the person who originated the material and indicate that the story needs to include more information regarding the program. Discover who the speaker will be for the next meeting, what she will be speaking about, and something about her credentials. Weave that information, together with the other answers to who, what, when, where, and why into the lead paragraph. Then take the subjective language the original writer is so proud of and rework it into a quote or two attributed to her. It has been surprising to me through the years how people can be somewhat easily impressed with themselves when they are quoted. In many instances, that will solve the problem.

The bigger difficulty is that such a solution is only short term and will probably need to be repeated with one person after another, month after month.

Forming a Parish Public Relations Committee

A long-term answer is needed, and that answer begins with an active parish public relations committee. Depending on the size of the congregation, the committee might have from three to seven members. It is probably best if the council appoints those members with the assistance of the pastor and the advice and consent of the editor of parish publications. Ideally, committee members are chosen on the basis of two qualifications: interest in the congregation's public relations program, and some expertise in communications.

The first person on the committee, but not the chair, is the editor of the congregation's publications. Others who would be good candidates are members of the congregation who are journalists, editors, published authors, designers, artists, and persons employed by the local post office.

Congregations that do not have these kinds of professionals available should look for people who regularly read newspapers and magazines, have an eye for good design, and maybe have even offered some opinions in the past about the congregation's need for a good communications program.

Empowering with Oversight

When a public relations committee is established, it should be empowered by the council (or by the congregation if the formation of the committee entails a change in the constitution) with oversight related to all of the congregation's communications projects.

If the stewardship, evangelism, education, or any other committees decide they have special needs for communication or public relations tools, they need to be encouraged to consult with the congregation's public relations committee for suggestions and assistance. That way, everything in the congregation's communications program will have a consistent, recognizable quality and style.

The public relations committee meets monthly in order to stay up to date with the congregation's communications needs, opportunities, and difficulties. The meeting agenda always starts with a critique of the past months' worship service guides, newsletter, posters, and special brochures.

The critique is a discussion designed to help the editor. Committee members might compliment the editor on the most effective stories, on the design and layout of the publication. They might also ask the editor questions about the choice of typeface, the readability of the text, the completeness of the information, why one significant story was given less priority than others, and why another story was omitted completely.

To be most effective, critique sessions must be supportive of the editor's efforts and at the same time ask legitimate questions that help the editor to improve future publications. Critique sessions that are perceived by the editor as being overly negative usually are not helpful.

Other items included in the critique might be general mailings to members of the congregation, indoor and outdoor bulletin boards, and street signage intended to help people find the congregation's place of worship. Committee members will also be aware of the congregation's e-mail and Web page services (see chapter 11) and will recommend improvements as necessary and appropriate.

Next, members of the committee might be shown the proposed tables of contents that have been developed for each publication so that they can make suggestions.

Editorial problems being experienced by the editor might be discussed so that the committee can either lend its weight in her support or suggest better ways to handle the situation.

Long term, the committee would make an audit of the congregation's audiences, audit the current communications program, and make suggestions regarding readability, size and style, mailing lists, frequency of publication, and possible reasons to add or subtract communications efforts now in effect (see chapter 5 and appendix A). The committee will also be aware of, or help formulate, the congregation's crisis communications plan (see chapter 9). (Note: if suggestions for change have an impact on the budget, a case for the changes must be submitted to and approved by the council.)

Finally, the public relations committee will want to work on suggestions for the working relationship between the editor and the writers, and help develop style sheets and guidelines for writing (see chapter 4 and appendix B). Eventually, the committee might want to sponsor a workshop for all writers and reporters and other interested members in the congregation.

Members of a strong public relations committee will also keep themselves informed regarding technological changes so that they can make appropriate recommendations regarding upgrades in necessary equipment and the congregation's electronic ministry (see chapter 11).

Settling Questions of Responsibility and Authority

Questions centering on the relationship between authority and responsibility are among the stickiest issues in how congregations deal with their public relations and publications programs. Competition, audience analysis, and techniques regarding improved readability and readership can all be dealt with through an improved communications philosophy, education, and technical expertise.

But questions focused on the relationship between authority and responsibility are questions of personality, power, and commitment, which makes it an even tougher battle. Nonetheless, it needs to be acknowledged, it must be faced, and it must be resolved. If the result of the discussion ties responsibility and authority together in the hands of the editor, a congregation's communications program will be better, and more of the congregation's people will be motivated to be servants of God.

It also will be a lot easier for representatives of the congregation to deal with the mass media. Congregations often seek media attention when they want publicity about special services and programs. Sometimes congregations would rather hide from public media when a crisis develops that might change the whole nature of their ministry. Those concerns are at the heart of the next chapter.

9

Relationships with the Public Media

Some ramifications of a congregation's relationships with public media have been dealt with in chapters 3 and 8. News release style and format has been illustrated in chapter 6. The basics of journalistic writing are outlined in chapter 4. Perhaps you are asking, what more can be said?

The positive connections that need to be made and nurtured between your congregation and the public media in your community—newspapers, radio stations, and TV broadcasters—cannot be overemphasized. You and the media do not have the same mission, but those media and your congregation are not adversaries unless you make them so.

Media make their mark by informing the people of your community what is happening to other people in the world—local, national, or international—around them. Religious organizations live to make public the good news of their creeds and scriptures and encourage and sustain people as their daily life demonstrates their faith.

First, a caveat. Relationships between congregations and media are decidedly different if your congregation is located in a large metropolitan area or if it is the center of a small rural town in western Pennsylvania or a relatively isolated landmark somewhere on the Midwestern prairie.

Metropolitan congregations have a difficult time getting into the "news hole" in the large newspapers and broadcasting stations that serve their members unless the media are looking for a special seasonal feature or some unusual news or conflict related to a congregation or its staff. (The news hole is all the space allocated for news, features, and photos after the sold advertising is in place.)

A growing number of metropolitan papers are including once-a-week "Faith and Life" sections, but even those special efforts—good, welcome, and positive as they are—cannot provide space for reports of a congregation's regular programs and ministry.

City and suburban congregations need to make connections with the network of smaller suburban papers that circle every major city. The editors of these community papers are hungry for stories that inform their readers about local events and interesting personalities in the neighborhood.

The editors of weekly papers serving residents of their small-town communities as well as farmers, ranchers, and hobby farmers in the surrounding rural country are also hungry for information about what is happening and who is making it happen. Usually these editors—sometimes without staff other than themselves—literally gobble up news releases from any organization or person in the circle of their readership and print them as they get them.

The program directors of small-town radio stations and small-market television channels are not quite as easily pleased only with written news releases, even though they will accept them. Their hunger is for other material that provides some kind of sound or picture possibilities that might enliven their broadcasts. Your congregation has an advantage if it provides "actuarials," short, high quality, 30-second audio tapes of a part of a speaker's presentation or a video clip of a special program.

Local radio stations across the nation air live broadcasts of hundreds of Sunday worship services every week for relatively small fees. If your local radio station has yet to do that with any other regular religious service, ask the manager, "Why not?" Then, after checking with the council and the pastor, introduce the idea that your congregation would be open to such a possibility.

Television stations usually are most interested in a connection with your congregation when they want to do a special feature focusing on the Christmas, Easter, or Hanukkah seasons or other religious celebrations.

But other stories might be even more powerful. Is your organist retiring after playing for every worship service for the past 45 years? Has one of your Sunday school teachers taught all the sixth graders in the congregation for the past 20 years? Has one elderly grandmother baked all the ethnic bread used by your congregation for the past 30 years in its annual Christmas season suppers? Was one of your teenage members who sings in the choir just named to the all-state basketball team?

Those are the kinds of stories that are the lifeblood of a congregation's history and tradition. And the local small town or suburban TV station might be interested in scheduling that story if someone in your congregation lets the program director know about it.

The bread-and-butter staple of news bureaus at many small colleges continues to be what is known as the "hometown story." Those stories focus on students on their campus—when they arrive, when they play on an athletic team, when they sing in the choir or play an instrument in the band or the orchestra, when they earn an academic honor, when they graduate. Basic information—name, hometown address, parents, year in school, academic major, special interests—is gathered with a short questionnaire during orientation after new students arrive on campus.

The writing of the release follows a simple formula and is often done by experienced student assistants in the college's news bureau office. But the payoff is huge. Nearly all small town and most suburban papers will run every one of those stories they receive, usually without changing a word of the news release, and they will also print the photo if one is sent along with the story.

Congregations in rural and suburban environments could get the same kind of coverage if they have a member who has the interest and training to spot the stories and do the reporting. But being involved in such a program is a tremendous investment in time and energy.

Fostering a Mutually Helpful Relationship

It is not enough to know the location, the phone numbers, and the e-mail addresses of the editorial office and broadcast studios of media in your community. You have to know the people, and those same media representatives need and want to know you. Communication—even communication through public means—is an intensely personal business.

As you get to know and appreciate the people, you also will become aware of the practical realities in which they work. What kinds of information do they want from you, and what kinds of information are of little interest? When do media need to know about the important events and programs in your congregation, and when is that information so late that it is beside the point?

Once you know the answers to such questions, you can help the leaders of your congregation get information to you in time so that you can respond to people in the media with appropriate material ahead of the media's deadlines.

It is counterproductive in the extreme to continue to try to feed media material that their representatives—reporters, editors, program directors—have already told you they cannot and will not use. And that is true even if you think they are horribly misdirected not to find such material interesting. It is also counterproductive if several people are trying to influence media about the same story.

The council should designate one person to be the media representative for a congregation. The pastor is often that person, but the pastor does not need to have that responsibility. Maybe the council could reach out instead to the congregation's publications editor or another media-wise lay leader from the public relations committee and appoint one of them as the contact person for the community newspaper and radio and TV stations.

Unwanted or unusable material ends up in the editor's wastebasket after a cursory examination. Too much unwanted material too often from the same source won't even get a reading.

Find out how the media want you (or another appointed media representative) and your congregation to help them. Do they prefer a news release on paper with an accompanying computer disk mailed through the postal system? Or is the disk not helpful? (There is no sense sending a disk if it is not going to be used.) Is a news release sent as an e-mail attachment preferred?

Would fact sheets be better than news releases? Fact sheets provide the five Ws, a note regarding the importance of the event, suggestions for possible photos or video, and the name, telephone number, and e-mail address of the one or two best sources for more information.

Faith group-related agencies and some large congregations send local media a page of story ideas and resources for story development once a month. Then the media personnel decide which stories they would like to see developed, who on their staff they want to develop them, or whether they want a story written by someone in the congregation.

Do the reporters interested in giving coverage to a congregational event appreciate a reminder phone call or e-mail a few days after they have received your news release? Or does that extra contact bother them, waste their time, and have a negative effect? Ask and they will tell you.

What are the deadlines for material for each of the media in your community? Once you learn them, note them and make sure the rest of your congregation's staff is also aware of them. Most of all, respect and adhere to them. Submitting a story or a story idea early is always better. Submitting a story too close to deadline is at best risky and at worst damaging to your relationship with the reporter whom you depend on for your congregation's coverage.

The Pastor as Resource

It is best not to make your pastor the primary resource for information in the contacts and stories suggested above. Occasionally, however, she is the one best qualified to answer questions. Sometimes, an enterprising reporter will want a quotation from the pastor on the significance of a program in the congregation. Then, obviously, the pastor is the contact.

Most of the time, however, an administrative assistant or a secretary in the congregation's office, or the editor of the parish newsletter and other congregational publications, is the best source for additional information wanted by a reporter. The pastor, with many other duties and concerns on her agenda, does not need to be bothered.

One major exception stands out, however, and in this exception the pastor is the primary resource. Clergy are often thought to be the moral compasses of their communities, a role they are comfortable with as the spiritual leaders of the faith groups they serve. But the responsibility goes farther than the membership of their congregations. The whole community looks to all of its clergy and other religious leaders to provide moral leadership and compassionate support whenever it is needed.

When a pastor moves into town to begin a new ministry, the staff member or other designated lay leader who has been the primary media contact from that congregation should accompany him on visits to all the media in the community. Make appointments in advance so that the editors and program directors have blocked out some time to become acquainted.

The congregation's media representative needs to have three things for each appointment: a news release announcing the arrival of the new pastor, a recent black-and-white or color photo, and an up-to-date vita or résumé. All the media are urged to keep both the photo and the resume for their files after they have run the announcement that the new pastor has moved to town. (Concerns about copyrighted portrait photos—a potential problem that can cause difficulties—are dealt with in detail in chapter 10 in the section, "Handling Copyright Complications.")

Now comes the good part. Somewhere in the introduction of the new pastor, he offers his willingness to be a spokesperson regarding the moral and ethical ramifications of community, national, and international news events.

Within the past half century, the religious community has had far too few spokespersons who are willing to relate publicly the essence of the faith of the congregations they serve to the day-in and day-out struggles for survival in their communities and their world. And too many of the people who have risen up as self-appointed spokespersons often voice a judgmental and uninformed theology far afield from the compassionate faith and ministry to which most faith groups aspire.

A new pastor, freshly introduced to local media personnel, can affirm that she is available to serve occasionally as a public commentator regarding such perplexing community issues as hunger, homelessness, environmental degradation, inadequacies in the school system, the loss of family farms, corporate fraud, abuse in families, sexism, terrorism, and war. Pastors, by the way, can and should also comment on more positive aspects of community life—new programs and facilities to help people who are hungry and homeless, shelters for abused people, the expansion of library programs, and the development of more playgrounds, parks, and other recreational facilities.

Conversations between pastor and media representatives can affirm that nearly everything that happens today on our community, national, and international stages has moral and ethical implications. Most of the time, unfortunately, those moral and ethical concerns are not made a part of day-to-day reporting.

More pastors need to say they are willing to help fill in that blank spot locally if asked occasionally for a brief comment on the moral, ethical, and faith-related implications of developing stories.

Most editors and program directors have not heard that kind of offer very often. Some will not take advantage of it when they do; others will welcome the idea and begin to figure out ways to make use of the offer.

Commentary on ethical, moral, and theological nuances in a local or national story can come in a variety of modes. It can be a short or extended quotation inserted in the story by the reporter or set alongside the story as what is called a "sidebar." It can be a signed letter to the editor. It can be a signed opinion column on the editorial page.

Mutual awareness of the same need for a voice from faith-based organizations can be an encouragement for the local ministerium to offer the media a monthly column—in print, on the air, or on videotape—dealing with the moral and ethical dimensions of current news. Participating members of the ministerium could create such columns on a rotating basis. Content could range from devotional thoughts related to the season to faith-connected reflections on the ethical ramifications of current social and political concerns. Many community ministeria already have such media connections and use them well.

Such programs carry some risks. But a thoughtfully written piece that points out relevant ethical and moral questions in current news without being doctrinaire or overbearing can be a tremendous help to readers who are looking for direction as they respond to what is happening around them. Taking that kind of risk on issues that matter in the daily lives of people is one way to answer those in the world who claim that religion today is irrelevant.

Being Prepared for a Crisis

Every congregation needs a crisis control plan. You hope you never need to use it, but if something happens with negative or traumatic connotations and it attracts media attention to your congregation or personnel connected with your congregation, a crisis control plan is invaluable.

The days we live in are rife with reports of scandals, indiscretions, and improprieties perpetrated by the leaders of faith-based organizations. Priests are accused of the molestation of children. Pastors are caught in adulterous affairs. Youth directors have sexual relations with teenagers. Clergy abuse their spouses. Financial officers skim the worship offerings. A member sues the congregation after injuring herself in a fall on an icy sidewalk.

All congregations hope such things never happen to them. But today's headlines too often reveal that all congregations—urban, suburban, small town, rural—are at risk for such abhorrent behaviors to affect them. It is bad enough if they happen, but it is worse if the congregation is not prepared.

Two almost contradictory responses are particularly important when representatives of the media begin to ask questions about something they "have heard."

First, face the questions head-on. If a leader of the congregation is guilty of what is being rumored, no amount of denial will change that fact. If the person is innocent of the charges, the facts, as they are made public, will prove that innocence.

Second, the questions of an inquiring reporter do not need to be answered immediately. It is perfectly appropriate to answer a reporter's surprise question for which you are not prepared by saying, "I am not aware of that situation. Please give me time to check out the story, and I will get back to you within the hour." Then get the reporter's phone number and make sure you respond within the time—even if you have to ask for more time to continue searching for the facts.

A Pattern for Your Crisis Plan

In anticipation of the worst, and in the hope that it is never needed, every congregation needs a crisis plan. Each congregation needs to design its own plan for dealing with crises that might catch them unawares. The plan should be in writing, and it should be reviewed annually or after any time that it needs to be used. Here are seven steps to include in your congregation's crisis plan.

1. Name the chief spokesperson
2. Write a statement for media
3. Develop lists of media phone numbers and e-mail addresses
4. Inform the judicatory office
5. Write a letter to members

6. Plan for the aftermath
7. Keep a detailed record

Now let's look at each of these steps in more detail.

Step 1: Name the Chief Spokesperson. It is critical for your congregation to have one spokesperson so that media hear one message from one voice regarding whatever issue is involved. Then the message will always be the same without fear of being caught in contradictory or conflicting comment.

It is also a good idea to designate a backup spokesperson in case the first is not available, or, in the worst of all scenarios, if the first designate is the person around whom the crisis revolves. In most congregations, either the pastor or the communications specialist on staff is the logical person to be the designated spokesperson.

Step 2: Write a Statement for Media. When a congregation finds out it is involved in a crisis of impropriety, scandal, confrontation, or physical disaster, someone needs to write a brief, standardized response immediately to answer imminent inquiries from the media. The statement should be cautious and intentionally brief. It does not attempt to accept or place blame or guilt, but indicates that people in the congregation are looking into all allegations and difficulties.

The response should acknowledge the problem and the congregation's concern, outline the status of whatever in-house inquiry is in progress, and if appropriate, list whatever coping mechanisms are already underway. If legal counsel has been retained by the congregation and is informed concerning the case, that person might also be named in the response.

The writer need not always be the same person for every incident. Depending on the problem when it first comes to light, one person on the staff might be more conversant with salient details than another, and the most knowledgeable person is the one who should write the first draft of the response.

Circulate copies of the initial response to everyone in the office, your legal counsel, and perhaps to the congregational president for their additional input and approval. Valid suggestions for change should be incorporated in the original document, but keep in mind that the statement needs to be clear and brief. It also should avoid elaboration on the situation. In other words, just the facts.

145

Copies of the revised response should be on the desk and easily accessible on their computer for everyone in the congregation's office and should be made available immediately to the president of the council and any other lay leaders who might be called by media reporters. Now, everyone in a leadership role connected to the issue knows what is being said, even if they are not authorized to be the spokesperson. Anyone in the office who answers a phone call from a reporter forwards that call to the designated spokesperson.

The standard message needs to be amended or added to and redistributed as more facts are revealed or the veracity of the original "facts" changes.

Of course, you have no control over any members of the congregation who might be interviewed "off the street" by an enterprising reporter. Most reporters, by the way, are innately sensitive to the concerns of a congregation in potentially embarrassing situations. The vast majority of reporters are not out to get you.

It has been my experience, however, that some reporters—particularly those connected to TV investigative teams—have a somewhat constricted conscience in these kinds of matters. For them, only the story matters.

Step 3: Develop Lists of Media Phone Numbers and E-Mail Addresses. The "easy contact" list of media phone numbers and e-mail addresses should be in hand well before a congregation is confronted with any kind of crisis.

Then, after responding to the reporter who made the first inquiry regarding the potential problem, and after you have the initial statement in hand, you are ready to be proactive and call or e-mail every person on the media list to give them the same information.

Do not, even for a moment, think that media who did not initiate the story are not interested in pursuing it. They are, and they will. It is best if they get the initial information from you.

When you call, most reporters will try to get more information from you than is written in your statement. That's their job. Resist the temptation to expand the story "off the cuff." If the questions seem to be legitimate, tell the reporter you will call back after you have had a chance to check those details. Then check the facts and call back as quickly as possible.

146

Step 4: Inform Your Judicatory Office. Your closest judicatory office needs to be informed of the situation as soon as possible. Update that office on all contacts made with the media up to that point and consult with appropriate personnel there regarding additional steps that need to be taken.

In most instances, the bishop or president and the communications officer will be able to provide counsel on next steps and give you support in other contacts that might need to be made.

Step 5: Write a Letter to Members. Almost nothing grows faster than the grapevine when crisis looms around an institution. Unfortunately, grapevine information almost always deals more with rumor, innuendo, and half-truths rather than with facts.

That's why it is critical to provide the facts as known to all members regarding every crisis situation in your congregation. Use your initial statement for the media as a starting point, describe steps that have been taken by the officers of the congregation and the judicatory, outline anticipated future action, and request their prayers for the least divisive and most beneficial solution to the problem.

The congregational letter must go out within the first two days after the problem has become public. Rumors form like a fog in troublesome situations within a congregation, and the sooner facts can be in hand to dispel half-truths and falsities, the sooner tendencies to form divisive factions can be dispelled. Do not wait for the regular issue of the periodic newsletter to publish the information; however, an update on the situation is appropriate in the first newsletter after the letter has been mailed.

A second letter to the congregation is often needed after the problem has been completely resolved. This might take the form of an outline of next steps in a rebuilding plan after a natural disaster. In cases of personal malfeasance, the second letter might be an apology from the offending party, carefully edited by another staff person to make sure that none of the content either intentionally or accidentally further inflames the situation or divides the congregation.

Step 6: Plan for the Aftermath. The problems of coping with and moving beyond natural disasters tend to follow a relatively simple pattern. The worship center burns down, blows away, or is serious damaged by a flood, decisions are made to rebuild or not to rebuild, and plans for the future proceed accordingly.

Problems of abhorrent behavior on the part of pastors or other congregational staff are much more complicated. The problems do not simply go away when the news coverage stops or the litigation has ended. Members of congregations have a tendency to take sides no matter how clear the facts in a case might be. Now is the time when a congregation really needs help from its judicatory officers.

Three kinds of help need to be provided, and they are all needed at once. The victim and his family (known or anonymous) need the uplifting hands of support and help in a painful and long-term healing process. The accused and her family need to find an atmosphere of understanding and forgiveness and the encouragement to move on. The congregation needs to remember that its members always include weak and frail persons who do not act consistently the way they are expected to and that the road to perfection is a winding and uneven one.

Without those kinds of understanding and supportive attitudes, congregations made fragile by unexpected turmoil can split into unreconcilable fragments. Some even die.

Step 7: Keep a Detailed Record. A complete record is essential to measure the effectiveness of your plan in the ways it helped you and the congregation to deal with the problem. It also provides benchmarks that will help you make your crisis plan more effective the next time it might be needed.

Keep a log of every phone call and every media contact. When was the call received? Who received it? How soon was a response made and what was it? What were the results in all media that picked up the story? What was the response of members of the congregation?

Both the office staff and the public relations committee should discuss everything that happened, the effectiveness of the plan in dealing with all contingencies, and together make whatever improvements are necessary. The governing board of the congregation should be fully informed of what happened, the resolution of the problem, and improvements incorporated in the crisis plan for future use.

If such concerns are not part of a congregation's crisis control plan, that plan is incomplete. At least some information regarding crisis plan improvements should be included in the next newsletter either as the subject of the pastor's letter or as a major news story.

Dealing with Tangential Difficulties

Some crises that affect a congregation appear at first only to be tangential. But they bring with them their own sets of problems.

Consider the possibility that someone in major trouble with the law is identified in the media as an active member of your congregation. It is hard to know why a reporter and an editor might think congregational membership and activity is germane to most stories about an arrest, but it happens more than congregations would like. And it is always painful when it happens.

More significantly, it feeds the frenzy of people who seem to take pleasure in pointing out the perceived failings of the faith groups and their members. Their accusations of "hypocrite"—"the church is full of hypocrites"—are hard for the leadership and other members of the congregation to bear.

The accused might be anyone: the organist who is sued for alienation of affection; the Sunday school teacher who embezzles funds from a real estate office; the teenage choir member who gets caught with a group that vandalizes a school; the council member who abuses his spouse; the choir director who is charged for the fourth time with driving while intoxicated.

It is not productive to try to make a public case against the media for the inclusion of what seems to be irrelevant information in the accused person's profile. When you know the reporter, editor, or program director, however, it can be useful to raise the question of relevance in a private phone call or face-to-face over a cup of coffee.

If the paper or station has an ombudsman on staff, that person also might be queried regarding the same concerns. But go to the person who wrote or produced the story first.

It is not possible for congregations to exercise an option regarding contact with the public media. Contact is going to happen. The only question that calls for an answer is, "Is that contact between congregation and media going to be mutually productive, or is it going to walk the thin, sharp edge of painfully nonproductive antagonism?"

Congregations and their leaders can work creatively and pro-actively to make their contacts with people in the media a productive and satisfying part of the ministry of stewardship, evangelism, social action, and communication. It takes effort and it takes understanding, but the results can be a mutual blessing. Try it.

10

Photography and Other Illustrative Material

The publication of the first issue of *Life* magazine in November 1936 demonstrated beyond a doubt the validity of the already old saying, "One picture is worth a thousand words." Thousands of uncounted photographs published in black-and-white and full color have verified that adage ever since.

Cameras changed dramatically throughout the 20th century—from large-view cameras that needed tripods to heavy speed graphic press cameras to 35 mm single lens reflexes (SLRs) to compact "point-and-shoots" to digital cameras that fit easily in a pocket or purse. But the goal of the photographer remains the same: to tell a story in the most dramatic way possible with a photo that needs few words to identify, describe, and explain it.

Parish publications can be enhanced and made more interesting and more attractive when dramatic photos are an integral part of their content. But that does not happen by accident. In fact, not many congregations have been able to make it happen at all.

In order for parish publications to be stronger competition for other publications in the market today, it helps if they can include some illustrative material. However, the difficulties are legion when trying to use photos well with the reproduction processes available to most congregations.

The first problem is finding or taking a photo that tells a story well, which is followed by the complications involved in inserting the photo in the parish publication to allow it to have maximum impact.

Finally, the editor is faced with discovering appropriate procedures and techniques that will assure good quality reproduction.

Shooting and Choosing the Storytelling Photo

Start with the basics. If a photo is out of focus (blurry and fuzzy), don't use it. If a photo is poorly exposed (too dark or too light), don't use it. If a photo includes people who are not easily identifiable (only the backs of their heads show or their positioning hides some faces), don't use it.

If the primary subject of a photo is so far away that faces are smaller than a dime, don't use it. Group shots of more than 10 people are always problematic if you cannot use the photo large enough to easily distinguish all of the faces. A better alternative to any kind of large group shot is simply to limit the photo to a small number of people from the group, or use a small, informal cluster, perhaps including one or two people who are key personages in an accompanying story.

If you are taking the photo yourself, or if you are helping to direct the work of a photographer, make sure the person, the activity, or the event is covered thoroughly. Photographers seldom get second chances. Review the photo possibilities suggested in chapter 6 for a groundbreaking ceremony for a parish education unit that involves children using the plastic sandbox shovels.

Plan for the event photographically by outlining possibilities you can anticipate. Going back to the groundbreaking assignment, the first shots on the list would be pictures of the children using their plastic shovels during the ceremony. You would also want pictures of the principal people in the groundbreaking service, including the pastor, the Sunday school superintendent, at lease one representative teacher, and the manager of the construction firm. You will also want photos of the others in attendance, particularly the reaction of the parents of the children doing the groundbreaking.

Make sure you or your photographer takes a variety of photos. They should include close-ups of one, two, or three participants, medium-range shots of participants and spectators when they are not individually involved in the main thrust of the action, and distance pictures of the large scene.

Always be ready for the unexpected shot of the child who grows shy in the limelight and who clings to his parents rather than joining the others in the groundbreaking action, or the assistance and disruption of a family pet in the proceedings.

Also note that whomever is serving as photographer should be encouraged to shoot a minimum of one 24-exposure film of the event. Actually, two or three rolls of film would be better. Then, even if not all the negatives are printed, they can be archived as a resource for future generations. Always carry at least one more roll of film than you think you will need. Remember that you will never have another chance to record an historic event. Given that fact, film is one of the least expensive materials you will use in all of your promotion and publications planning.

Regarding the question of color or black-and-white film, with current technology good color prints will reproduce as black-and-white pictures in your parish publications just as well as if you used black-and-white original prints. Even though black-and-white negatives and prints still have a longer archival life, it is harder now to find black-and-white film on the retail shelf, and even more difficult to find a processor who will develop and print it.

Making the Shift to Digital Photography

If the photographer is shooting with a digital camera, discussion of film and processing is of little consequence. Start with the appropriate image card for the camera being used. Processing can be handled in several ways. The card can be taken to a photo shop that can provide 4 by 6 inch glossy prints together with a CD-ROM of the entire photo collection (the disk is useful for future reference since digital photography does not provide any negatives).

It is less expensive to have only the CD-ROM made first with a proof sheet, then to choose only the images from which you want prints made. Even better is to edit the card in the camera before any of the images are copied by deleting everything that is obviously below standard and unlikely to be used.

Or, the card can be downloaded in the office of the congregation on a computer with the appropriate program. Then prints can be made as they might be wanted, and all the images you decide might have value can be filed and stored. Pictures selected for use in the newsletter can then be edited and set in place by the computer, either for the next issue of the newsletter or for a publication 10 years in the future.

Every congregation today should consider investing in a good quality digital camera to be used exclusively by members of the staff for congregational events. The cost of digital photography has dropped dramatically since the turn of the century. A good camera can be purchased for $250 or less. Buy two memory cards with a minimum capacity of 8 MB (bigger is better), as well as two rechargeable batteries so you always have a good one in hand when the one in the camera dies.

The interface cable that allows you to transfer your photos from your memory card to your computer should come with your camera. Make sure everyone who might use the camera reads the instruction booklet thoroughly with the camera in hand and goes through the basic processes with someone who is experienced in operating the equipment.

To make the congregation's digital investment complete, it is a good idea to buy and install Photoshop, a photo-editing computer program that helps you crop a photo, change its size, rotate the picture, and even manipulate colors, shadows, and subjects (more about photo editing toward the end of this chapter).

Photoshop is a relatively expensive program with a rather steep learning curve, but once a member of the staff becomes conversant in its operation, it can be the best way possible to make initial preparation of photos—digital or otherwise—for inclusion in a congregation's publications.

The transition from traditional photography to digital is not difficult, but it does have a few niceties and complications that can sneak up on the first-time user. Let's look first at the niceties.

- Digital cameras come with both a viewfinder and a monitor and you can use either one to see and frame the picture as you take it.
- As long as your memory card is big enough, you don't have to worry about running out of film. (I have taken more than 150 images on one 96 MB CompactFlash card.)
- You can check the photo you just took immediately on the monitor screen to see if it is what you want. If it is not, shoot more of the same scene until you get the best possible picture. Then you can delete the poorer, unusable photos, opening up that space for other pictures.

- Processing can be as fast as the time it takes for you to get back to your computer plus a few minutes, which can be even faster than traveling to your closest one-hour photo service and picking up the pictures an hour later.

Complications are minimal but they can be bothersome.

- Many digital cameras have a delay of a couple of seconds between when you press the shutter release button and when the shutter actually activates and the flash lights the scene. The delay can be frustrating when you are trying to catch fast-moving action or candid expressions. Practice and honing your sense of anticipation, however, can help to solve the delay problem.
- Care is called for when reviewing images on the monitor and deleting poor pictures. An instant of carelessness while working with the functions menu can delete everything on the memory card rather than only the image you wanted to get rid of. Speaking from personal experience, once that happens, everything starts over. It is a horrible feeling. You get no second chances to reclaim deleted images.
- Printing pictures from the memory card yourself is complicated without additional equipment to supplement your word processor printer.

Selecting Photos for Publication

Once you have photos in hand or in your computer for use in your parish publication, it is necessary to make some choices. Which are the best quality pictures? Which best tell or enhance the report of the event? Which will reproduce the best?

Your choices gravitate to the good quality photos that tell the basic story of the event without the need for much additional text. The standout photo will have dramatic impact, showing strong emotional and personal involvement and interrelationships in connection with whatever event or occasion is being reported.

If enough photos have been taken, a few photos almost always will stand out as the best. Limit your choices to those. Sometimes an event is so big that several photos are needed to reflect the full scope and significance of the occasion.

But what about all those photos you took that do not meet this criteria? What do you do with all the extras? First, identify all of the prints by writing information lightly on the back of the photo with a number-two pencil or ballpoint pen. Work on a firm surface, and do not press hard on the back of the photo with the pencil or pen. Too much pressure forces the impression through the print and pushes out the surface on the emulsion side. When that happens, the impression of the pencil is permanent and will show on the face of the photo.

Post all the photos you are not planning to use on a bulletin board, number them with a tag near the print, and put up an order form on which people can order prints for their personal scrapbooks. Make sure you check how much reprints will cost first, and offer the ordered pictures for that cost plus whatever fee you think is reasonable to cover the handling of the orders. You might be surprised at how many parishioners will take you up on your offer with multiple orders for their family scrapbooks.

Editing Photo Space Effectively

Now to photo editing. Whether your photos are "old fashioned" prints or digital images, you still need to make important decisions to use this illustrative material most effectively. Note figures 1 through 3 below. They illustrate use of formal portraits or less formal head shots. What is needed to move from figure 1 to figure 3? Two things: enlarge the image and crop (trim) the margins.

Figure 1 illustrates the composition of many formal portraits. The person is centered in lots of space. Consequently, the size of the face—

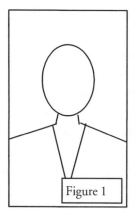

Figure 1

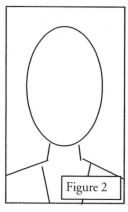

Figure 2

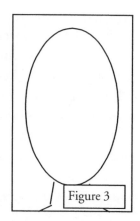

Figure 3

the only part of the portrait your readers are interested in—is relatively small. Note how that space around the face has been cropped away in figures 2 and 3. The frame of the picture (the total space used) remains the same, but the face is made to be much larger, much more easily identified, and much more interesting. Figure 3 illustrates the best use of a portrait in a parish publication.

Another common photo used not only in parish newsletters but also in publications of nonprofit organizations is what is known as the "grip and grin shot."

Two people stand next to each other, shaking hands in congratulations as one of the people holds a check, a plaque, or a trophy. Most editors look on the subject matter as deadly. Some will not even consider using a grip and grin photo because it has become a standard cliché, usually posed somewhat woodenly and completely lacking in spontaneity.

A better illustration is a picture or series of pictures showing the honoree doing some of the things that earned her the honor, or a series of photos showing the donor with the people who will be helped by the donation. Be that as it may, some of the most common problems with grip and grin shots can be solved if the photographer is aware of them and thinks out their solutions in advance. See the illustrations in figures 4, 5, and 6 below.

The problem in figure 4 started when the photo was taken. Notice how far apart the two figures are. All that space between the heads is wasted, which you cannot afford if you are editing the limited space in a parish newsletter. The photographer who took the picture needed to be assertive enough to say something like, "Please get closer together.

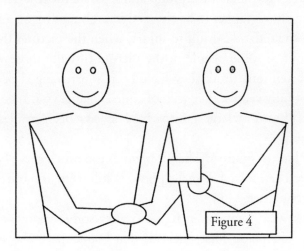

Figure 4

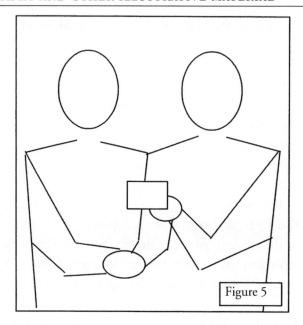

Figure 5

When you stand so far apart, it looks like you don't even like each other."

In my experience, people simply do not like to be close to each other when their pictures are being taken. But if you take group photos (even of only three people) you sometimes almost have to lose a bit of your civility to get members of a group to arrange themselves with the shortest people in front, overlap their shoulders, and get in a position where they can see the camera lens. ("If you can't see the lens of the camera, it won't be able to see you.") For larger groups, it is mandatory that the photographer finds a place that has a wide staircase or other means to elevate parts of the group and separate the rows. It is also useful for the photographer to be elevated several steps up on a stepladder.

Even then, to add insult to injury, when the pictures they ordered are sent out, if some people in the picture (usually those who would not pay attention) think they have been shortchanged because their face is not fully visible, they will, of course, blame you. It goes with the territory. Photos of large groups have always been my least favorite assignments.

Now look at figure 5. The problem of too much space between the people has been solved. But the photo is still using too much space for the subject matter.

Check what happens in figure 6 after some creative editing and cropping take place. First, most of that blank space above the heads

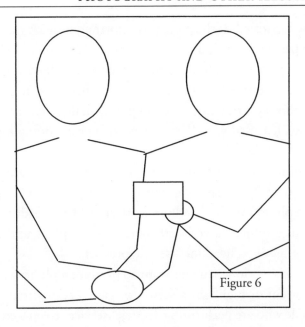

Figure 6

and below the hands has been removed. Second, the extra space left and right of the people has been taken away.

Now, in slightly less space than figure 5, the material remaining in figure 6, pared to the essentials, presents the same information without any distractions around the perimeter and with faces that are about 50 percent bigger. The impact is immediately more dramatic. Consequently, the final picture is more interesting.

All the principals involved in cropping the grip and grin shot are applicable to any other photo that you might include in your parish publication. Simply ask yourself when beginning the photo editing process, "How much of this picture do I really need to include to tell the story?" Then crop until the photo matches your story.

One last hint on cropping. Be aware of perpendicular lines and straighten the primary up-and-down mark in the center one-third of the photo so that it is at right angles with the top and bottom of the picture. Commands in Draw, Photoshop, and PageMaker programs all make the straightening procedure relatively easy.

Using Photo Space Creatively

Editing and cropping the photos you want to use in your publication is one challenge; placing them is another. First, every photo you use deserves to be identified. If the picture is a portrait, it needs to have the name of the person (often only the last name is adequate) under the photo. If it is a grip and grin, the people need to be identified (left to right) as well as the event that makes them so happy. If it is a more complicated photo portraying part of an event, all the identifiable people need to be identified as well as how what they are doing relates to the event.

Second, if a photo is not accompanied by a separate article, the identification (usually called a caption or a cutline) should include a headline. The photo caption headline works just like a headline on an article. It needs a subject, a verb either stated or implied, and usually an object. (For more on headlines, see chapter 4.)

But what do you do when you want to produce a photo feature to report on an event or highlight a season or give special attention to a group of people who are performing a special service? Keep a couple of guidelines in mind. First, select three to five photos (an odd number always seems to work best) that tell the story. Keep scale (close-ups, medium range, and more distant shots) and variety (a small group of people, one person, the setting without people, a close-up of the end product) in mind when making your selections. Be aware that only a part of a photo will sometimes have more impact than the whole.

Now you are at the point of layout. Scale and variety are important here, too. One photo should be larger than the others to dominate the design. Some can be horizontal, some vertical, and remember that a square format can also be attractive. Also, make sure you leave space for a headline as well as text that identifies all the photos, either in a few narrative paragraphs or in cutlines.

Note that the examples in figure 10-7 and figure 10-8 are all done on an 8½ by 11 inch page formatted for two or three columns. The same process can be adapted for use in any format, including 8½ by 7 inch or 8½ by 5½ inch. The smaller the format, however, the smaller and less dramatic the scale.

Also note that the headlines are all indicated to be in boldface, all text is in regular serif typeface, and the cutlines are all in italic. Those differentiations, subtle as they seem, are one more nicety that helps the reader through the page. You do not need to use these suggestions, but it is important to be uniform of your use of type for different kinds of content.

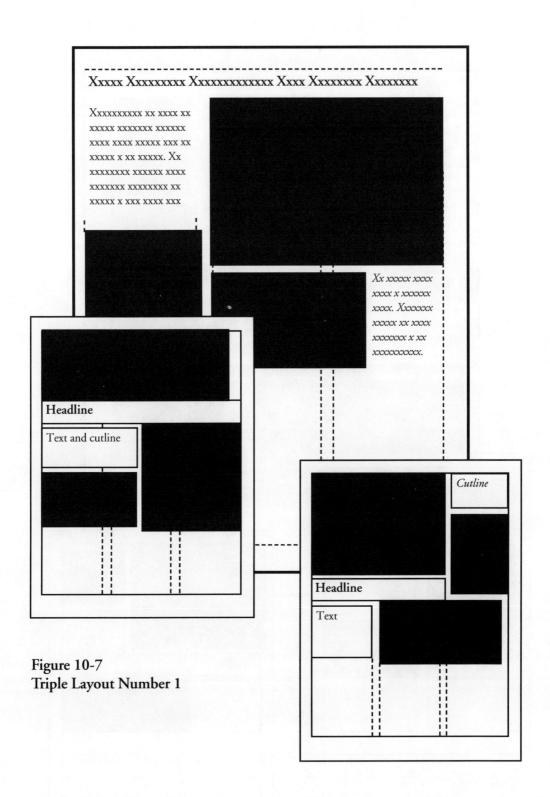

Xxxxx Xxxxxxxxx Xxxxxxxxxxxx Xxxx Xxxxxxxx Xxxxxxx

Xxxxxxxxxx xx xxxx xx xxxxx xxxxxxx xxxxxx xxxx xxxx xxxxx xxx xx xxxxx x xx xxxxx. Xx xxxxxxxxx xxxxxx xxxx xxxxxxx xxxxxxxx xx xxxxx x xxx xxxx xxx

Xx xxxxx xxxx xxxx x xxxxxxx xxxx. Xxxxxxx xxxxx xx xxxx xxxxxxx x xx xxxxxxxxxxx.

Headline

Text and cutline

Cutline

Headline

Text

Figure 10-7
Triple Layout Number 1

161

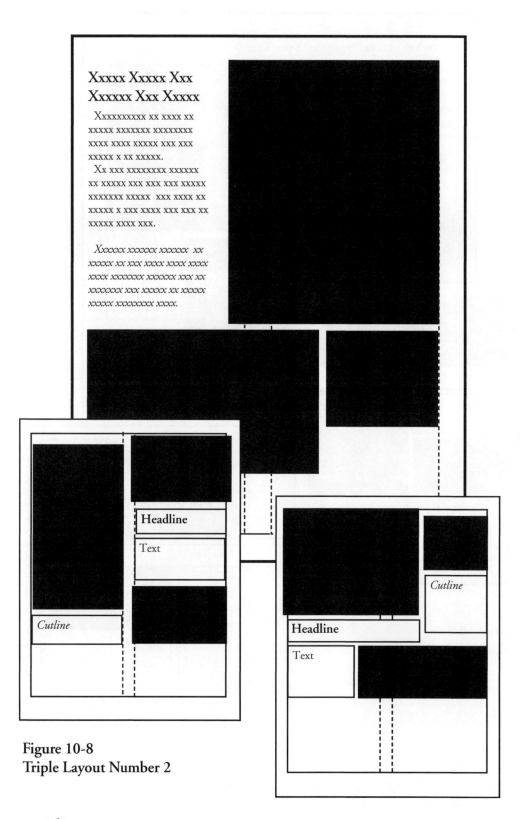

Xxxxx Xxxxx Xxx Xxxxxx Xxx Xxxxx

Xxxxxxxxxx xx xxxx xx xxxxx xxxxxxx xxxxxxxx xxxx xxxx xxxxx xxx xxx xxxxx x xx xxxxx.

Xx xxx xxxxxxxx xxxxxx xx xxxxx xxx xxx xxx xxxxx xxxxxx Number xxx xxxx xx xxxxx x xxx xxxx xxx xxx xx xxxxx xxxx xxx.

Xxxxxx xxxxxx xxxxxx xx xxxxx xx xxx xxxx xxxx xxxx xxxx xxxxxxx xxxxxx xxx xx xxxxxxx xxx xxxxx xx xxxxx xxxxx xxxxxxxx xxxx.

Headline

Text

Cutline

Cutline

Headline

Text

Figure 10-8
Triple Layout Number 2

162

One more look makes it apparent that in some layouts, photos are placed to intentionally violate the margins—a good way to expand the size of the photo and give it more dramatic impact. The only caution is to make sure you know how close to the edge of the paper you can go before your copier will be unable to reproduce the material. It is also important to limit how often you break your established margins. If you do it too often, the reader loses track of where the usual margins are and the procedure loses its graphic impact.

The only remaining concern is how to finish the page. First, leave at least three-eighths of an inch of space between the bottom of the photo layout and the beginning of text in all columns. Then you can use either a one-, two- or three-column headline to introduce the next story. Ideally, that story (or stories) would be complete in the space available at the bottom of the page.

Sometimes, you might want to reverse the order and put the photo layout at the bottom of the page with a longer introductory story or any other related material at the top. If you need ideas, check photo layouts in current newspapers and magazines. Do not be afraid to borrow and adapt the layout ideas you see there at will.

Dealing with Professional Artists, Designers, and Photographers

Sometimes a publication project is so important in the life and ministry of a congregation that the publications editor, in concert with other leaders, needs to think about the possibility of hiring professionals. The work of professionals in the field of art, design, and photography stands out from similar efforts by amateurs. Professionals can and will discover and solve publication program problems that you might not even have known you had. But be aware of certain procedures when you call on professionals for assistance.

First, establish timelines for production in advance. When does the finished product need to be delivered? When do you need to see preliminary sketches from artists and designers? When will you and other involved staff make decisions regarding alterations to the approved art or design sketch, and when must the finished art be delivered?

With photographers, you need to agree early on to the philosophical approach to the assignment, the people who will be the best subjects to illustrate that approach, the settings or locations where the photos will be shot, and the size and kind of photos you need as finished prints. Also, will the photographer work alone, or does she want you or your representative present when the photos are being shot?

A word of caution: if your assignment for a professional—be it photographer, artist, or designer—is too specific, it has a tendency to take away some of the creative energy you are paying for. If it is not specific enough, the artist, designer, or photographer does not have adequate guidance to produce what you want and need. Conversation about purpose, intent, mode of production, and anticipated use of the finished work is essential before the assignment is contracted.

Also make sure that the costs and method of payment, as well as the deadlines, are spelled out in advance in a written contract. Professional art can be expensive. With the right conversation in advance, it can also be made to fit limited budgets. But never try to negotiate costs after the work has been completed.

You will also want to ask other questions before signing a contract. Does the finished work belong to the congregation, or does the artist continue to maintain some control?

Can the work be used only for the publication for which it was planned, or can the congregation use it for additional purposes such as supplemental brochures, bulletin covers, an art print that might be offered for a limited edition sale later to members?

It is well worth the expense to bring in outside professionals occasionally to provide creative artistic help to a congregation for special communications projects. But make sure you have thought out exactly what you want and need well in advance, make sure the creative talent is clear about those needs, and be certain that all details regarding deadlines, costs, and related concerns are spelled out in a written and signed contract.

Handling Copyright Complications

One complication that is sometimes overlooked is the question of who owns the copyright on the work of a photographer, artist, or designer. Does purchase of the art include purchase of a copyright release, or does the copyright continue to be held by the person or firm that did the creative work? It you face that question, negotiate the purchase of a copyright release with acceptance of the work.

One example: If your pastor has a publicity portrait taken by a local professional photographer, the photographer usually retains the copyright. Consequently, unless a copyright release is purchased, the original photographer must make all duplicate copies of the portrait needed for the office publicity file, often an expensive proposition.

Over the long term, it is a good investment for the pastor (or the pastor's office) to buy the copyright release when the photo is taken. The copyright release fee usually is relatively modest—about 25 dollars. Once the release has been purchased, reproductions can be made (usually less expensively) wherever you want and whenever you need them.

Keeping Up with the Technology

One more consideration needs discussion. It does not matter how good your photographs are or how creative the layouts if your copy machine cannot reproduce them well. Photographs are more than black and white or dark and light. Photographs are filled with gradations of gray (256 tints) that go from absolute black to absolute white.

All photographs must be scanned before they will reproduce well. A good scan should have a range of 3 percent black in the highlight (white) areas to 95 percent black in the shadow (darkest) areas. The quality of the scan is known as its resolution. A good resolution for printing is 300 dots per inch (dpi). A resolution of 300 dots (also known as pixels) in every one-inch square of the scan provides all the detail necessary for good reproduction in parish publications.

Photos printed on copy machines without first being scanned lose the gradations of gray and reproduce only in absolute black-and-white tones with uneven, untrue, and unattractive blotches in between. Black-and-white material is reproduced in publications as either line art (type and most clip art) or halftones (photos and other art). The shades of gray in all photographs cannot maintain their detail when reproduced as line. Even color photos reproduced as black and white will be transposed into a grayscale.

Look carefully with a magnifying glass at a black-and-white photo in any newspaper, and you will see a series of dots (the line screen in which it was printed). The larger the dots, the darker that part of the picture; the smaller the dots, the lighter that part of the picture. Solid black sections have no dots, only solid black ink. Solid white sections have no dots at all.

The dot patterns are made by halftone screens that turn all blacks, whites, and the middle gray tones into a series of dots, the line screen in which the photo in the publication was printed. The highest quality reproductions in the most sophisticated publications use 175 to 200 line screens (lines per inch). Newspapers usually use an 85 line screen.

If you plan to include reproductions of photographs in your parish publications, you need access to a scanner (to copy photos into computer files) and a copying machine (to reproduce photos in your publications) that can print photos in half-tone screens. Otherwise, it is almost impossible to avoid the blotchy reproductions of photographs that show up in far too many newsletters.

If such equipment is not available in your own office, and budget restrictions will not allow any upgrading of equipment in the near future, try this alternative. Visit a copying services center, let the people there know your concern about good reproduction of photographs in your parish publications, and ask them what procedures would be best for you to get the kind of reproduction you want.

Take along copies of the photos you plan to use in the publication, printed and cropped in the size in which you want to reproduce them. The photos should be trimmed to size with a straight edge and a sharp knife or razorblade. (If you have the Photoshop computer program, you do not have to trim the original photos but can crop them yourself after the halftone images have been made.)

Have the copying services center scan the photos for reproduction with an 85-line screen and transfer the images to a disk. Take the disk back to your office, file the images in your word processor, and move them into the places where you want them in the layout of your publication. The results will be dramatically different and incalculably better.

Trust the people at the copying services center to help you find the best and most economical solution to your halftone reproduction problems.

Contemporary Photography's Moral Dilemma

About two decades ago questions regarding moral and ethical dilemmas related to the use of photography hardly ever came up. Concerns related to good taste were sometime discussed, but they seldom flowed over into moral and ethical questions.

Today, however, with the possibility of relatively easy digital manipulation, photography has become one more moral and ethical battleground.

Go back to the discussion of grip and grin shots and the problem of too much space in the photograph between the principal participants. It is not all that difficult for a talented person, working in the Photoshop computer program, to take the photo with the extra space, delete the space electronically, and thereby move the people closer together. That accomplishes the same thing as taking a second photo with the people closer together. But is the digital manipulation moral and ethical?

Look at another possibility. A photo you want to use of several members at work in the church kitchen has a messy counter in the background. You are sure that messy counter would be an embarrassment to the people in the photo. You can clean that counter off completely with digital manipulation. But should you?

A group shot of 10 people who are members of an important leadership committee in your church includes a person who dropped off the committee after the picture was taken. That person's image can be taken out of the photo without anyone except the people in the picture knowing the difference. Should that be done?

Or how about this question? Some telephone and electric poles, together with the usual wires and cables, make it impossible to get a clear and uncluttered photo of your church building. However, all the poles and wires can be removed digitally to create an absolutely unobstructed view of the building. Should they be?

The ability to manipulate images is a gift. Shadows can be deepened or made lighter. Colors can be muted or intensified. Unsightly backgrounds and foregrounds can be eliminated. People can be added or removed or moved within groups. Use the gift, but remember that every decision you make which changes the way things were or are has moral and ethical overtones and undertones. Be cautious.

One way to answer the moral and ethical questions regarding possible photo manipulation is to ask another question: "If I were in the photo, and an editor's change of details in that photo involved all or part of my picture, would I be concerned, offended, or embarrassed?"

If the answer is yes or even maybe, you have just stumbled over the moral and ethical issue. That means it is unlikely that you will mess with the potential manipulation.

The Use and Abuse of Clip Art

Many congregations produce parish publications filled to overflowing with little pieces of "art" clipped from voluminous libraries of clip art available in their computer. Some editors, it seems, have never seen a piece of clip art they did not like.

Some clip art can be used effectively. Too much of it, however, is borderline "cute." And cute denigrates the communications purpose and mission that should be the underlying foundation of most parish publications. Remember, good design is meant to communicate, not decorate.

Here are a few guidelines for use of clip art.

First, use it with restraint. You do not need clip art on every page. Good writing and good graphics will attract just as much attention just as fast as a single piece of clip art. Any page of a newsletter that includes more than three clips of art will automatically look like an unplanned mishmash. It draws the reader in too many directions at once, provides priority for nothing, and takes space away from substantive text that could have been more informative, educational, and motivational. Few pieces of clip art have any informational, educational, or motivational value.

Second, if you think you must use clip art, search for the piece that has some obvious relevance to the subject matter of the story to which you are trying to attract the reader's attention. Clip art only for clip art's sake can be self-defeating.

Third, do not use clip art with words and phrases as a headline or heading for the story that follows. Too often, the words are so buried in the drawing that they get lost in the reader's translation, and they do nothing to set the stage for the substance of the stories they are intended to introduce.

Fourth, keep it current. Clip art that is more than a decade old allows readers to disconnect from your intended message. Outdated art and archaic hair and clothing styles get in the way of clear communication.

Fifth, if you feel compelled to use multiple pieces of clip art on the same page, choose material that has a compatible artistic and design style.

If clip art is to be used, the secret to its effectiveness is the quality of the resources from which you choose the material. Search the Web—it is full of good material that your congregation can buy as either a book or a CD-ROM. You will find many sources. A few are still free, but most of the good ones require some payment.

While a list of Web pages that could supply clip art might be useful, such lists go out of date quickly. Some Web pages I suggested initially when this book was being written were no longer available by the time it was published.

However, a search on the Web for "Clip Art for the Liturgical Year" (or variations of that theme) will bring up a list of as many as a thousand sites where you might find the kind of material that suits your tastes for use in your parish publications.

Illustrative material, well edited and well reproduced, can be a major asset to parish communication. Poor illustrative material, whether it is a badly reproduced photograph or clusters of inane clip art, can be a severe liability. The good stuff promotes readership. The bad material gives potential readers an excuse not to take the communication seriously.

Be alert to the value of good illustrative material, and make your editorial choices accordingly.

11

Moving to Electronic Ministry

Amazing changes have taken place in communication in recent decades, and hardly a month goes by without the demonstration of either a new electronic breakthrough or an upgrade in tools and systems already in use. A few people still try to resist the tides of change. Some congregations continue to hold on to the tried and true but achingly archaic modes of communication they have struggled with for years.

Some procrastinate about joining the electronic age because they are immobilized by what sounded like financial horror stories regarding costs decades ago, and they have not checked back with computer companies or retailers since. Others live in perpetual intimidation, sure that a word processor would swallow page after page of their priceless prose—whether it is a sermon or the copy for a newsletter—and every word would have to be re-created all over again.

With the possible exception of the youngest among us, whether we are pastors, secretaries or other staff, or lay leaders in congregations, most of us have been plagued by such misgivings at least once in our life. Most of us have taken the plunge into the deep waters of electronic communication and the exciting new mode of ministry it makes possible. A few have had to come up for air a couple of times, but none have drowned, and most are swimming quite successfully and enjoying the electronic waters so much that they wonder how anyone now survives without them.

Those who still think only in terms of computer-related financial horror stories have not looked recently at how word processor prices have tumbled, even as electronic capacities and capabilities have gone up. The intimidated ones have never learned that it is almost impossible to lose something completely unless a person really wants to.

They also have never had the joy of moving pieces of text around without re-keyboarding any of it, changing whole paragraphs from subjective to objective with a few keystrokes, breaking large blocks of text into several paragraphs, or adding more current and up-to-date information without rewriting the entire report.

I recently had a conversation with a man who had a computer and Internet connection in his home but would not try to use e-mail or search the Web. Adamantly, he claimed, "There is nothing on the Web that I want or need to know." How sad. The real reason, I think, is that his typing skills are at best rudimentary—a situation that can be remedied.

Even more unfortunate: he has far too much company. It is tragic when people cut themselves off from whole new worlds of information because they feel intimidated by the technology that they are afraid to try, or think they need just one more skill they have not yet learned.

The Changing Demographics of Electronic Usage

It is useful and important to consider some demographics, but keep in mind that these statistics change quickly. The Pew Internet & American Life Project (www.pewinternet.org) reported on September 9, 2001, the results of interviews with 26,094 adults 18 and older between March and December 2000. According to that survey, 56 percent of all Americans went online (used e-mail or the Web). By age categories, 75 percent of those who were 18 to 29 years old spent time on line, 65 percent of those 30 to 49 years old, 51 percent of those 50 to 64, and only 15 percent of those over 65 ever went online.

The percentages of online usage increase every year, but the ramifications are significant for congregations and the people they can expect to reach effectively through Internet communication and ministry.

At the same time, however, according to a Pew Internet Project report dated December 23, 2001, 28 million Americans use the Internet to get religious and spiritual information and connect with others regarding faith-related experiences. After the Twin Towers tragedy of September 11, 2001, in New York City, 41 percent of Internet users said they sent or received e-mail prayer requests. The Internet can

171

certainly be used as a supplemental tool to enhance religious beliefs and commitments.

Take a look at a news release from the Pew Internet Project published a year earlier on December 12, 2000. It was headlined, "Congregations Say the Internet Helps Their Spiritual and Community Life." The dateline is Washington, D.C. The news release reads:

At a time when some worry that the Internet is isolating users and replacing traditional communities with virtual ones, a new survey by the Pew Internet & American Life Project suggests that many churches and synagogues have found new energy and purpose through use of the Internet. Most of the 1,309 responding congregations say their Web sites and e-mail use have helped the spiritual life of their faith communities and bound members closer together.

The findings in this holiday-season report, "Wired churches, wired temples: Taking congregations and missions into cyberspace," show that many congregations offer a wide array of material on their Web sites that range from simple brochure-type material such as directions to the church to space for prayer requests to features that allow global mission work.

"These responses show that e-mail and the Web are being used by many real, not virtual congregations to sustain and deepen their members' faiths, to enrich their worship, to evangelize, and to fulfill their missions," says Lee Rainie, director of the Pew Internet Project. "These very traditional places tell us that their use of these 21st Century technologies has made a difference for the better."

This study by the Pew Internet Project is believed to be the first extensive quantitative effort to discover how churches and synagogues in the United States use the Internet. This is not a representative sample of all the congregations in the United States because it comes from people who voluntarily responded to an e-mail invitation to fill out an online questionnaire. However, the wide-ranging and extensive responses of churches to this survey suggest that the Internet has become a vital force in many faith communities:

- 83 percent of those respondents say that their church's use of the Internet has helped congregational life—25 percent say it has helped a great deal.

- 81 percent say the use of e-mail by ministers, church staffs, and congregation members has helped the spiritual life of the congregation to some extent—35 percent say it has helped a great deal.
- 91 percent say e-mail has helped congregation members and members of the staff stay more in touch with each other—51 percent say it has helped a great deal.
- 63 percent say e-mail has helped the church connect at least a bit more to the surrounding community—17 percent say it has helped a lot.

The report itself contains an extensive list of Web addresses for congregation Web sites that illustrate a wide range of features.

Some 471 of the respondents to the survey were ministers and rabbis, and they were asked about their own personal use of the Internet. "A striking number of the clergy at these churches have turned to the Internet to get material for sermons, worship services, church education programs, and their own personal devotions," says Elena Larsen, the Research Fellow at the Pew Internet Project who authored the report. "They use the Internet like many others as a vast library in which to hunt for material that matters most to them."

Most of the respondents are eager to use their Web sites to increase their presence and visibility in their local communities and explain their beliefs. They are much more likely to use the Web for one-way communication features such as posting sermons or basic information about the church, rather than two-way communications features or interactive features such as spiritual discussions, online prayer, or fundraising. The most commonly used features on these Web sites are:

- 83 percent encourage visitors to attend their church.
- 77 percent post mission statements, sermons, or other text concerning their faith.
- 76 percent have links to denomination and faith-related sites.
- 60 percent have links to scripture studies or devotional material.
- 56 percent post schedules, meeting minutes, and other internal communications for the church.

The Pew Internet & American Life Project is a research center funded by the Pew Charitable Trusts. The Washington-based project will explore aspects of the Internet that have not received sustained attention from policymakers and commercial research firms: its effect on children and families, communities, schools, the work place, and civic and political life.

So, where does the congregation you serve fit into this picture?

Elevating E-Mail

The instant communication possible through e-mail is almost a necessity today for effective ministry. Think of the possibilities. First, put a brief request in your parish newsletter for members of households to e-mail their congregation's office with their e-mail addresses.

The number of members with e-mail capability might vary from 10 to 85 percent, which should not matter. Begin with what is possible, and include periodic requests in your newsletter to update and enlarge the list every three or four months.

The requests for addresses might also include a question regarding whether those connected to the Internet would like to get their copies of the newsletter and other parish publications on e-mail or whether they still want copies on paper. If members say e-mail is their preference, then you might want to send a message to those people alerting them to the fact that the newsletter has just been posted on the congregation's Web site. Then prune and organize your postal mailing lists accordingly to save the costs of sending the printed publications to those homes.

Once you list members' e-mail addresses in your e-mail address book as "new contacts," you can organize them into "new groups." Your first group is "Congregation," which includes everyone. Then you probably want groups for "Council," "Youth," "Women's Auxiliary," "Men's Organization," "Choir," a separate group for each of the boards, "Ushers," "Altar Guild," "Catechetical Class," and "Public Relations Committee."

Don't forget a group listing for "Prospects" (include spaces for e-mail addresses in your guest book and visitor registration cards to get the information) with the hope that the congregation can move many of those e-mail addresses into the "Congregation" group fairly soon. "Media" should, of course, be a separate group (see chapters 3 and 9).

Think of the potential once you have those lists, particularly if a high percentage of the congregation has e-mail. Reminders of meetings, practices, and rehearsals can be distributed with a quickly typed note and one click of the "send" command. Only those without e-mail need to be phoned.

Think about this. If your congregation were fully wired, sending out notices of meetings and events by e-mail could even cut down on those ubiquitous bulletin inserts discussed in chapter 7. Announcements and reminders of bake sales, potluck dinners, ski trips, catechetical class assignments, midweek worship services and their accompanying soup and bread suppers, and vacation Bible school and Bible camp registrations could reach the bulk of a "wired" congregation with efficient effectiveness.

If only a few in any group do not have an e-mail address, wired members might volunteer to call those who are not in the e-mail group.

One additional e-mail concern needs to be addressed. I have been surprised to discover that some congregations have only one e-mail address for everyone in the office from the pastor to the custodian, which sets up an unnecessary lack of privacy among the staff.

Most e-mail providers have arrangements that make it possible for a congregation to have a single e-mail account with several separate and private e-mail addresses that can be accessed by individual passwords. The supplemental addresses can be set up at no additional cost. If your congregation does not have that kind of system, call your Internet service provider to have it changed.

Making the Most of the Web

Congregational Web sites are exciting new modes of communication, but you do not have to look at very many to discover the need for better use of the medium. Most denominational Web pages now include lists of the Web sites of all their member congregations and are easy to access.

A look at only a few of them alerts you to major problems. Photos are too large, thus taking too long to download. People's faces in the photos are too small and not easily identified. Colored ornamental backgrounds and large blocks of reversed type get in the way of easy readability. Lines that are too long and sans serif typefaces in large blocks are too tiring to read.

Most of those problems can be solved easily. Simply apply the same recommendations for readability emphasized in chapters 4, 5, and 10 for publications printed on paper.

But first, we have to talk about getting the development of your own congregation's Web page under way if it does not already have one. Perhaps you are one of those fortunate congregations in which a member (often a teenager) has experience in designing Web pages. If so, tap that talent, even if you have to pay a fee for the service.

If that kind of resource is not in your congregation's membership, check the Web page of your national denomination. Many of them offer instructions for getting started and templates to make the beginning work easier. Also, Web page software can be purchased, and someone on the staff can work their way through it, setting up the congregation's Web page as they go. The learning curve might be steep, however, and the effort will undoubtedly be time intensive.

If none of the above possibilities seems to be workable, you probably need to go to a full- or part-time Web designer. But once you have made the contact, find out exactly what services such designers will and will not provide and exactly how much it will cost. Also check to see how much training the designer might provide for a member of the congregation's staff so that the Web site can be kept up to date in-house.

But no matter what method gets your congregation's Web page underway, the most important thing (if your congregation is not already on the Web) is to get your page started. It will never happen if you wait for the perfect time, because every time will be something less than the best time for the beginning of what seems like such an imposing task.

Listing Potential Content

Whether you are going to do the page in-house or are bringing in help, begin by developing a list of potential content. The following is a list of content suggestions.

- Full name and address of the congregation, with the logo and typeface that you are using in all other publications and public relations efforts. Make sure your e-mail address is included so visitors to the site can contact your congregation easily for more information, and make sure someone in the office where e-mails are received checks them regularly so that inquiries are answered the same day they are sent)
- A map and narrative directions to help people find the congregation
- Days and beginning times for worship services, Bible studies, and other education programs, and auxiliary groups that meet regularly
- Introductions of the pastor and other staff of the congregation
- A brief history of the congregation, including its denominational affiliation
- A brief introduction to your faith group's theology, including a listing of sacraments and other sacred rites
- A list of organizations, how each organization serves, and opportunities for membership
- Introductions of officers and other leaders of organizations
- Meditative material such as a prayer for the day or week, scriptural references, and the sermon theme and outline for the upcoming worship service
- Music material such as the anthems to be sung by choirs and hymns to be sung by the congregation during the next month's worship services
- Announcements and invitations to all events for the upcoming month
- Information regarding the seasons of the liturgical year and the significance of the colors of the paraments and clergy vestments
- Selected articles and notices from the most recent periodic newsletter
- Photos of the building, staff, and groups of people in worship, Sunday school, or other activity sponsored by the congregation

All of this material needs to be put together in creative ways that attract and hold potential viewers. Here are some suggestions.

- Use color photos, not black and white, and keep them relatively small (not more than 2½ by 4 inches). Larger photos make the

177

site download more slowly, and if viewers get impatient they will move on without waiting.

- Keep text short, with a maximum word count of 250 words per subject. Less than 250 words is even better.
- Use an informal, objective writing style that presents an inviting and welcoming congregation.
- Make sure the site can be "navigated" easily with a well-defined and easily understood menu on the home page and repetition of menu subjects on each subsequent page.
- Some form of patterned movement in a photo, a logo, or other art helps to hold attention; however, it also increases download time.
- Broaden the site's usefulness with links to the national and area judicatories, local social-services agencies with which your congregation has a connection, and maybe the site for the local community where your building is located.
- Enhance your site with color, but do not let the color overwhelm your material.
- Sound the first bars of a familiar hymn to set your site apart from many others.

Once your Web site is designed and you are satisfied with what it says, how it looks, and how easy it is to navigate, you need to take one more step. Make sure your Web site is listed in search engines and directories so that it comes to people's attention as a resource when they are looking for information on faith groups and how congregations might be helpful to them.

Your Web designer will be able to get your site into the appropriate lists. Additional information together with offers for free sites can be found at Search Engine Monitor Pro (www.searchenginemonitor.com).

Defining and Avoiding Potential Problems

Web page problems show up all too quickly when you begin to surf through some of those listed in denominational home pages. Study them, note the qualities of the ones you like, and analyze the problems that raise barriers to good electronic communication in the ones that are less than satisfying. Then make sure your congregation's Web page does everything it can to avoid those same difficulties.

Note that if something curtails readability on the printed page (see chapters 4 and 5), the same readability problems are accentuated on a computer screen. Here are a few of the more common problems to be avoided.

- A text-only site with no photos and dull colors.
- Photos of large groups where people cannot be identified.
- Excessive use of sans serif type that is too small in lines that are too long.
- Too many fonts in too many sizes.
- Large blocks of text reversed in black or bright colors.
- Patterned backgrounds that take too long to load and decrease readability.
- An overly subjective use of language for all subject matter.
- Out-of-date material. (I recently looked at one church's Web page in which all of the calendar material was 10 months old. Sadly, it was useless.)

Once your site is "live" and is being updated regularly, log on to it yourself at least once a month to make sure it is as accessible and up to date as you expect it to be. On one recent surfing expedition, while randomly looking at unfamiliar Web pages, I happened upon some sites that could not be accessed at all. Others were "under construction," some included a great deal of distracting advertising, and some could be accessed only as a link in the Web site of the city where the congregation is located.

With increasing frequency, your Web site is the first view a new family in your community might have of your congregation's ministry. It sets up the first impression. It can be the welcome sign and the invitation to membership. It initiates the first visit and provides information for continuing active membership.

Congregations can no longer ignore the call to electronic ministry. It is here to serve, and it is here to stay. Grasp the potential of that call and acknowledge it as a gift of communication as important in this 21st century, as Johann Gutenberg's movable type was almost five centuries ago.

12

Celebrating Special Events

Congregations mark their life and service by the benchmarks of special events. Building programs, organizational restructuring, and the introduction of new programs that substantially change the mission and ministry of a congregation can all serve as "igniters" for a revival of spirit and action.

And the audiences for these igniter moments can go far beyond the membership of the congregation. Special events, communicating ongoing faith, life, and vitality, can have a positive effect on prospective members. With the help of reports in the media, they also make a strong positive impression on citizens of the larger community that surrounds a congregation. Special events always offer opportunities to retell the congregation's mission and history in new and broadened contexts.

Among the most dramatic of these igniter moments stands the celebration of an anniversary. Whatever the number of years to be celebrated, anniversaries are significant. They demand attention, and that attention must be well planned, well in advance of the celebration. Consider one dramatic example of successful advanced planning.

The Cathedral of St. Paul in Minnesota began a $35 million restoration at the turn of this century. The edifice had been built nearly 100 years earlier in the first decade of the 1900s.

Significantly, the people involved in the planning of this project thought well into the future as well as the past. With the enthusiastic participation of the construction company, nearly 70 hours of the restoration work was videotaped with the use of a "cathedral cam." Much of that material was divided into a series of "reflections" linked to the cathedral's Web site. In addition to the record of the restoration, the reflections also included interviews with many of the workers and artisans involved in the massive project.

All of that videotape, shot over the course of the 30-month restoration, was masterfully edited into a one-hour special titled "A Crowning Achievement," which not only included interviews with the workers and artisans, but also with priests and parishioners whose lives have been touched by the cathedral. The program was a marvelous mixture of the current restoration as well as clips of historic people and events through the cathedral's nearly century-long life.

"A Crowning Achievement " was seen in an estimated 84,500 households when it was shown during evening primetime (more than twice the expected audience) by the local Public Broadcasting Service (PBS) affiliate in the Twin Cities in early January 2003. VHS and DVD versions of the video were offered for sale by means of a trailer at the end of the program.

That is what vision and long-range planning can accomplish. Not every congregation—in fact, not many—can afford the costs of such sophisticated reporting. But the point is that far too few congregations use their innate creativity far enough in advance to do any part of this kind of celebratory project. Part of the problem is that they simply do not have the vision to think big enough to take full advantage of opportunities that might be at hand.

Nothing in a congregation's celebration of its life and ministry is beyond the supporting reach of its programs in publicity, publications, and public relations. If it is happening, it cries out to be noticed. And if a happening is to be noticed, communication is at the core of the planning and the event. And the people responsible for the publicity, publications, and public relations programs—be they pastor, newsletter editor, public relations committee, or combinations of all of those resources—must be involved in that planning.

Getting the Planning Underway

So where do you start if your congregation has a special event on the horizon? Let's begin with an anniversary. At least three years in advance of the anniversary date, an anniversary committee needs to be formed and begin meeting on a regular basis. Committees can take many shapes, but one that works well for anniversaries employs a strong sub-committee structure.

A few years ago, the senior pastor of the congregation where I am a member asked me to chair the 125th anniversary committee. I saw the request as a fascinating opportunity, but also one that would be a tremendous challenge with the potential for an inordinate amount of work over the next three years. But I agreed to take on the assignment if I could pick most of the committee members and set up a committee structure designed to spread the work around equitably.

The anniversary committee structure depends heavily on a cluster of subcommittees. Here's how it works.

Every member of the anniversary committee is the chair of a sub-committee. Each chair picks her own subcommittee of about five members. If some members are more popular because of their abilities and their willingness to serve, the first subcommittee chair to ask them gets them.

Subcommittees will vary from congregation to congregation, of course, but standard subcommittees might include:

Anniversary Gift Subcommittee

Congregations have an unusual opportunity to make a major benevolence gift in addition to their regular annual benevolence contributions in conjunction with the celebration of an anniversary. Do not let the opportunity go by unanswered. Celebrations of congregational anniversaries are times of vision and thanksgiving as well as remembrance. All three motivations can be tied together when a congregation commits itself to make a substantial anniversary gift that looks forward to future challenges while remembering the ministry of the past.

Additionally, a special anniversary fund offers a challenging opportunity in communications. First, the fund is a living demonstration of the proportional stewardship on the congregational level to which its members are called on an individual level. It also moves the celebration of an anniversary away from the idea that this event is locked only in the past and only in the congregation. The anniversary gift speaks loudly about the congregation's response to the present and future needs of individuals and institutions apart from the celebrating congregation.

The ramifications of a substantial gift given by a congregation celebrating its own anniversary are significant in any communications program. First, members of the congregation, while participating in such corporate benevolence, are also having the theology of proportionate giving nurtured and reinforced in their personal stewardship.

Second, opportunities for communication about stewardship are enhanced and emboldened. Members talk to each other about what their congregation is accomplishing as part of the anniversary celebration. The leadership of the congregation talks to its members through frequent articles in the monthly newsletter that report on progress, encourage continuing participation, and provide examples of the people and programs that are being helped through the significant extension of the joy of celebration. The congregation witnesses its mission to its wider community through news stories relating through the public media the accomplishments of the special giving program. The anniversary gift is, of itself, a celebration that can start a river of positive communication to all of the celebrating congregation's constituencies.

History Subcommittee

Most congregations are surprised by how little is known about historical specifics when they begin to plan their anniversary celebrations.

The history subcommittee might need either to establish or to activate an archive, search the memories of older members for historical details, and identify other sources such as the local newspaper office for verification of names and dates.

Would the local historical society be interested in sponsoring a public exhibit open to the community on the history of the congregation?

Ministry and Mission Subcommittee

How has the mission and ministry of the congregation changed during its history? What impact have such changes had on the congregation's place in the community?

The ministry and mission subcommittee might develop lists of pastors, organists, choir directors, council members, and sons and daughters of the congregation who have gone into full-time service.

This subcommittee might also invite former pastors and other leaders back to the congregation as guest preachers, banquet speakers, or forum leaders to help celebrate its history.

Education Subcommittee

What changes have taken place in the education programs of the congregation? How have curricula changed and why? How many children have been taught throughout the congregation's history, and how many teachers taught them?

Who has served as directors of education, and who has taught children and adults in the congregation's education programs? The education subcommittee ferrets out these facts and proposes creative ways to celebrate them.

Music Subcommittee

How and when should the congregation's ministry of music—the choirs, the organists, vocal soloists, instrumentalists and instrumental groups—be involved in the anniversary celebration?

Can lists of former organists and choir directors be developed? Should any of them be invited back as participants in the anniversary celebration? Should a series of recitals or mini-concerts be scheduled to showcase individual musicians who are or have been members of the congregation?

Does the congregation have musicians in its membership who might be commissioned to write and compose a special anniversary anthem? The music subcommittee proposes plans that focus on the celebration of music throughout the anniversary remembrance.

Other Arts Subcommittee

What arts and artists in addition to musicians have been involved in the congregation's history? Should some of them be featured in the celebration?

Maybe the congregation has enough artistic talent among its members to sponsor public exhibits of members' art and folk art. Should a limited edition art print be commissioned for sale?

Does the congregation have the resources for the preparation and mounting of an exhibit of historical photographs? The other arts subcommittee searches out the artists in the congregation and proposes ways those special gifts can be celebrated as part of the anniversary observance.

Event Arrangements Subcommittee

How many anniversary banquets or similar celebrations should the congregation sponsor and when? Should former members be invited back, and if so, how can mailing lists for invitations be developed?

Do these celebrations need themes, and what should they be? Are the banquets going to be catered or potluck? Can the banquets be held in the congregation's facilities, or does a bigger hall need to be rented? Should tickets be sold for the banquets, or should admission be free?

The event arrangements subcommittee deals in details and how those details can enhance anniversary celebration events.

Promotion and Publications Subcommittee

Can a series of historical vignettes be developed for the local newspaper or radio and TV station as well as the parish newsletter? What's the best way to keep the schedule of anniversary events in front of the membership? What anniversary events should be announced to the wider community?

Should an anniversary logo be developed and who should be commissioned to create it? Are special anniversary banners needed? Should an anniversary book be produced? If so, who writes, edits, and designs the book, where will it be printed, will it be free or for sale, and when will it be published?

The promotion and publicity subcommittee needs people who are writers, editors, designers, photographers, and publishers. Most congregations do not have all of those kinds of people among its members, but take what is available and do what is possible.

If professional communicators are available, the anniversary committee can approve the recommendation of the promotion and publicity subcommittee and be confident that the tasks will be done and done well. On the other hand, if professional communicators are in short supply among members, the anniversary committee might want to suggest that some of the work of anniversary communication be done in close consultation with the newsletter editor or the congregation's public relations committee. Regardless of personnel, the promotion and publicity subcommittee will want to establish a long-range schedule for its publications and media relations.

What is the delivery date for a published schedule of events to be distributed to members of the congregation? What kinds of historical feature stories can be developed for the local newspaper or radio and TV stations and what is the optimum time for them to be published, heard, or shown? When will a series of historical vignettes begin to run in the parish newsletter? Who will develop and write them? Might the personal stories and faith-related experiences of some members—old and young—of the congregation be developed to supplement historical vignettes in the parish newsletter and the public media? If so, who?

The list of publicity possibilities goes on and on in a celebrating congregation, and the legwork needed to make it all happen is almost mind-boggling. Members of the promotion and publicity subcommittee need to either be or find resources for the foundation work of celebratory communication.

The list of tasks and talents can be nearly endless. Who are the writers? Who can conduct and make a record of interviews? Who will work through archives and unorganized documents for interesting historical facts? Who will uncover personal stories related to the congregation's history and get permission to use them? Who will contact media representatives to find out what might be most useful to them? Who will conduct the search for historic photographs, and who will make sure the anniversary celebration is adequately documented on film? Who will develop ideas for TV coverage? Finally, who will keep track of all the assignments, draw together the creative work they produce, and put it together with some form of editorial consistency?

Pastoral Support

One member of the pastoral staff (ideally, it should be the same one at each meeting) serves as an ex officio member of the anniversary committee.

A big bonus with the subcommittee system suggested above is the number of people in the congregation who become intimately involved in the planning for the celebration. Eight subcommittees are suggested above. If each subcommittee has five members, including the chair, that's 40 members of the congregation who have been given a vested interest in the anniversary celebration.

Involvement means participation. Participation means excitement. Excitement creates commitment.

Helping the Committee to Function Efficiently

The chair of the anniversary committee convenes and conducts the meetings, keeps a record of committee decisions and actions, sets the agenda, serves as liaison to the council or board, and helps committee members to have fun and enjoy each other's company.

The first meeting of the anniversary committee sets the stage for the rest of the committee's work. The role of each subcommittee is spelled out so that everyone knows where the lines of responsibility lie, the differences in those responsibilities, and the need for each group to bring recommendations to the anniversary committee early.

Every subcommittee recommendation is approved, approved with alteration, or rejected by the anniversary committee. No subcommittee recommendation is ever dismissed without discussion.

Questions of scope must be addressed. How long will the anniversary celebration last—a weekend, a week, a month, a year? What date should mark the celebration highpoint? Since major anniversaries (50, 75, 100, 125) do not come along in a congregation often, the celebration might deserve to be stretched out over a relatively long interval of time.

A major component of the communications program for an anniversary celebration is the development of an overarching theme. Move in the direction of a two- to five-word phrase, probably biblical, which relates not only to past growth and success, but also to future challenges.

Once a theme has been picked, the committee needs to decide on whether or not an anniversary logo should be developed. Anniversary logos are not necessary, but they add a degree of sophistication to celebration activity. They also help to provide a consistent, identifiable image in the design of anniversary materials. (See chapter 13 for more information on logo development.)

Questions of the range of the anniversary committee's authority must be addressed. What kinds of decisions regarding activities, calendar, costs, and budget have to go before the council, and what decisions can be made independently?

Introduce the question of the anniversary budget. Will the congregation set aside money in its annual budget for anniversary celebration? If so, how will the sum to be requested be calculated? If not, how will capital be raised to finance the celebrations that are planned?

Considering the Production of an Anniversary Book

Anniversary books involve work, but once produced, they are invaluable congregational resources. Once again, the mantra is "plan ahead."

The first decision that the anniversary committee needs to make is: "Do we want to make an anniversary history a part of our anniversary celebration?" If the answer is yes, the committee needs to decide how it wants to get the job done. One way is to delegate supervision of the work to the publicity and publications subcommittee.

At least four choices are available, depending both on the anticipated size of the project as well as the training, talent, and willingness of capable people in the congregation.

- Commission a member to write, edit, design, and supervise production.
- Commission several members to work as a team to produce the book.
- Commission a member to serve as editor and select other members to write brief essays on the history of various aspects of the congregation's life and work.
- Hire a freelancer from outside of the congregation to write, design, and deliver the finished history.

Whichever way you choose, invite the editor to anniversary committee meetings occasionally to report on progress and relate any problems that might be creating difficulties. The editor should also be encouraged to work closely with the promotion and publicity subcommittee and make use of the historical material that is being developed there. While the purposes of an anniversary subcommittee on promotion and publicity and the editor of an anniversary history are not the same, they certainly overlap and the material that each one uncovers and develops might be useful and instructive to the other.

The question of payment is important. Many people—particularly those who are members of subcommittees—do a great deal of time-consuming work as a voluntary labor of love. However, if the anniversary history is expected to be an amply-illustrated 150-page book covering the past century, that task will take more hours than most members who are fully employed can afford to volunteer. In fact, the editing of a congregation's anniversary book can be a three-year project.

Consequently, a congregation needs to consider the advisability of hiring the anniversary book editor. If an editor is to be hired, a contract should spell out general expectations for the anniversary history that will be produced and the delivery date, as well as the amount to be paid. The contract might also include suggestions on how sophisticated the publication might be (number of ink colors, number of photographs, quality of paper, size of pages, and type of binding) so that the book remains within its budget.

Payment for the work involved in producing a congregational history does have a major advantage. When you pay for a creative product, you have control over the finished material. If it does not meet expectations, then you need not use it. Or, you can insist on specific alterations before you accept and pay for the product. The contract between the congregation and the creative resource makes it a professional relationship.

On the other hand, if the work is strictly volunteer and no payment is involved, saying no to the work that has been done—or even calling for major alterations—is at best difficult and at worst disastrous to the relationship with that hardworking volunteer who might unknowingly have stepped into something over her head. That philosophy holds true whether you are dealing with writers, editors, designers, or composers. Unfortunately, when someone tries to get something for nothing they too often end up with nothing that can be used.

Whatever organizational structure is used for the person or persons given the task of producing a congregation's history, answer all questions of who has responsibility and who has authority in the same ways suggested in chapter 8.

Whomever is commissioned or hired to produce an anniversary history, the time and effort that person will expend on the project depends to a large degree on the resources already available in the congregation. If an archive that has been cataloged with care for the past 50 or more years is available in the congregation, much of the work is already in hand. Unfortunately, that is unusual.

Lacking a well-kept archive, the next resource is the congregation's office files where you should be able to find copies of bulletins, newsletters, and the minutes of all council and congregational meetings, all filed in chronological order. Those files are invaluable, but they are also inadequate for a comprehensive history.

Next, try your local paper. Every paper keeps an alphabetical "morgue" of clippings of past stories. That file can provide the facts about major events in your congregation's history—the arrival of new pastors, the dedication of buildings and building additions, and announcements of special services. Obituaries of long-time members might be illuminating, but they can also be a resource with limited value.

The Importance of Oral History

Even if a well-kept archive is available, the most interesting resource is the oral history that can be provided by interviewing the congregation's oldest members or others who have been members for long spans of time. Two things are important when making those interviews. First, develop a set pattern of questions that identifies the people being interviewed, their home addresses, how long they have been members, and what leadership roles they might have played in the life of the congregation. After that, let the conversation roam wherever the information they provide takes you.

Second, always use a tape recorder. Some people get a bit tight lipped when a tape recorder is introduced. However, after the interviewer lets the person know its use is needed to make sure the record of the interview is accurate, he can lay it on a nearby table or chair and not fuss with it again except to change the tape. The tape recorder will soon become an unobtrusive and forgotten part of the scene. Once the conversation is on tape and labeled, it becomes part of an expanding file of oral history.

One resource that might be useful for gathering oral history is older teenagers in the congregation. Once they have been briefed in terms of what kind of information is needed and what special insights are hoped for, interested teenagers can be major assets in the interview process. They will often pursue story lines that older interviewers might take for granted. The bonds of friendship that can develop between the older and younger generations as a result of the interviews are a bonus for the congregation.

Transcribing tape to text is tedious and time consuming. An editor might want to have someone else do that. Once transcribed, the editor will want a hard copy as well as a disk of the interview that can be filed in her computer for possible incorporation into the text of the anniversary history.

Excerpts from interviews can be used effectively as "sidebars" or brief descriptive text that sheds light and warmth on the body of historical information. The sidebars can be boxed and scattered throughout the book. Each box might include a candid photo of the person who was interviewed.

Organizing the Editorial Team and the Content

Organizing the information to be included in a history is hard work—even for good editors. Start with an outline. That outline will expand beyond your wildest imagination as your research uncovers more facts and as interviews point you in unexpected directions. As you begin to fill in the details with text, you will find yourself moving sections around, changing the order, revising the emphasis. Note that chapters do not necessarily have to be chronological. History outlines can be built on a framework of separate chapters for different areas of a congregation's life and ministry with each chapter wrapped around its own chronology of achievement.

Never forget, however, that the creation of a congregational history is a team effort even if you alone have been commissioned to get it done. One copy should go to the congregation's office for review. Another copy should be read by one or two people in the congregation noted for their precision and attention to detail. Their job is simply to check the facts, catch any inconsistencies, and suggest remedies for possible omissions.

Photos are another potential problem for many church histories. Too often, the photo file in the archives is frustratingly thin. If that's the case in the congregation whose history you are trying to produce, put out a plea for photos that might illuminate the congregation's history. A brief article—perhaps you will need several—in the newsletter will often pay off with a variety of old photos from family albums.

Make sure whoever receives them records the name of the person who supplied them so the photos can be returned. If the person who brings the photos in can also identify them, that's an unusual bonus.

The quality of old photos from members' family albums will be uneven at best. Technology can come to your rescue once again. Photocopying machines in many discount stores can often print a new copy for you that will be larger, clearer, and cropped better than the original. In many stores, the price is now under 10 dollars for four different 4 by 6 inch prints on the same page. Other photo resources include the files of your local newspaper and your local historical society.

As you work on choosing what historical events to feature, you will come to the conclusion that you cannot print a book big enough to include all the information you will find. As you decide what photos to include (if you are lucky, you will be able to include only the best of many) make sure your design plan includes plenty of white space.

Your congregation's anniversary history book will be eminently more readable and interesting if both the words and the pictures are uncrowded and have room to breathe. Review chapter 5 where the material on formatting bulletins and newsletter applies to bigger publications as well.

Choosing and Working with a Printing Company

If possible, choose a printer who is located in your hometown or in a nearby community. This can be good public relations for your congregation to keep the work close to home. It is also easier for you to work more closely with a local printer where you can solve editorial and design problems together (and it will be most unusual if you do not have editorial and design problems).

If the printing firm you choose knows that the scope of your project is beyond its capability, it will suggest other nearby printing houses that could handle the job.

Writing and Dealing with Specifications

If several printers are available in your community, write up a set of specifications and call for competitive bids. The specifications must include the number of copies you want printed, the page size, your estimate of the total number of pages, an indication of the quality of paper you desire for both the cover and the inside pages (ask for samples with their bid), how many colors of ink, your approximation of the total number of photos and other art, whether you will be providing the text on a computer disk or as hard copy, and the time and place that you need delivery.

Be careful about changing or adding to your original specifications when one of the printers asks for more information. The questions might be legitimate, but if you give additional or different information to one printer bidding on your history book, you must contact the others and give them the same information. Otherwise it will be difficult for you to judge the bids equitably.

Whether you call for bids to determine the printer or whether you simply go to the only printer available in your town (perhaps the owner is a member of your congregation), make sure you and the printer agree on all costs and charges before that printer begins work on your congregation's anniversary history.

Once you have chosen your printer, work closely with that firm to fine-tune answers to questions about size and layout. A good printer, even in small towns, will be able to offer many options for your choices in paper, ink colors, and the most economical sizes and bindings.

You might decide to go to a standard page size for books of 6 by 9 inches. That size, however, severely restricts the creative use of photos. The larger 8½ by 11 inch format provides 17 by 11 inch double-page formats that give you the option of dramatic photo layouts. Also ask your printer about options for binding, together with their costs.

A Bit about Bindings

Binding refers to the way the book is put together. "Edition binding," the traditional method for hardcover books, involves sewing the pages together at the bound edge. "Perfect binding" holds the pages together with a flexible adhesive. "Saddle-stitch binding" fastens the pages together with staples on the fold. "Mechanical binding" uses either a plastic or metal coil to hold the pages together.

Perfect binding is the most elegant for thin books because it provides a flat spine on which the name of the book can be printed. However, depending on the thickness of the paper and the capabilities of the printing plant, any book of less than 80 to 100 pages will probably need to be saddle-stitched.

Readability Rules Still Apply

Review the rules for good readability in chapter 5 regarding line length, font choices, and type size. Also check the photo layout guidelines in chapter 10. All of those suggestions apply just as much to a congregation's history book as to periodic newsletters and worship service folders.

Considering Color

Consider having your book printed in two colors throughout—black plus a brighter tone. Ask your printer how much more it will cost and let the firm's technicians give you ideas for how you can get the most out of the second color ink. Your printer can show you a mind-boggling collection of possible colors in the Pantone Color Formula Guide (also known as the PMS book).

One important hint: the basic reading color should be black or a very dark blue or brown that has a high percentage of black in its mix. The second color needs to have enough substance to be seen easily by itself. Pale yellows, golds and oranges, light tans, soft pinks, and light blues seem to fade into the paper and usually do not work well as second colors because they lack dramatic impact. On the other hand, blues, deep reds, reddish browns, burgundies, purples, and greens can all give dramatic impact as second color accents.

Combinations of screens, solids, reverses, and duotones (ask your printer about this process and how it is applied to photos and other art) can make two-color printing look like much more when used creatively.

Living with Your Logo

If the congregation has an anniversary logo, use it frequently—maybe as often as once on every two-page spread. Also use devices such as extra-large capital letters at the opening of major sections and smaller initials to break up the text in most columns. Study some of the more sophisticated magazines to see what they do to make pages look interesting, and feel free to borrow their ideas.

Taking Advantage of Technology

Let technology save you money. Once you have all the copy written, and trusted proofreaders have checked it (do not forget that you can distribute everything you write and edit by e-mail), you can carry the text of the entire book to your printer on disk. That way, you do not have to pay the printer to have the material keyboarded a second time. It also makes proofreading much easier since that work was already done before the text was sent to the printer.

If you have a computer program such as PageMaker, you can also format the entire book and send that formatting to the printer on disk. However, it is probably best to have the printer turn photos into half-tone screens and insert them in the places you have suggested in your layout. Most personal word processors cannot produce the half-tone screens that will provide the best photo reproduction in a book (see chapter 10).

Additional Content Ideas

Two other ideas for possible content take a lot of time and demand extravagant attention to detail, but are interesting additions to the telling of a congregation's history. The first is a timeline that puts events in the history of the congregation parallel to a second line that identifies events in the world and nation, and a third line that gives the chronological history of the community where the congregation is located.

The second idea is to include lists of people who have made a difference in the congregation. The lists might include all the congregation's pastors, all the international missionaries supported by the congregation, all the congregation's organists and choir directors, all the members of the council through the congregation's history, and all the sons and daughters of the congregation who have gone into full-time service in their faith community. If you decide to include these kinds of lists—and maybe even if you do not—you need to include a caveat somewhere in the book's opening pages. That caveat might read:

> The lists that go back the farthest never existed before this publication. It is certain they are scarred by omissions and have errors in their dates. The first names of many of the early missionaries remain a mystery, particularly of the married women. Don't take offense.
>
> Many members of the anniversary committee and their subcommittees worked on this information to put together the best lists that existing records and memories allowed. But some of the early recorders did not pay enough attention to reporting the objective information historians yearn for. Please report any error or incomplete information to the church office so that the record can be corrected for the future.

Answering Questions of Distribution

The only thing left is distribution, for which you have several possibilities. Some congregations budget the anniversary history book as a gift to all member units. When the printer delivers the finished copies, members who attend worship can pick up the copy for their family. This plan, however, calls for some sort of check-off system so that you know which families have their books and which ones need to have their copies delivered to them. The advantage of this plan is that every family receives a copy of the history; the disadvantage is a rather hefty budget item.

Some congregations avoid that problem by soliciting sponsors for the publication of the book, with names of all sponsors listed in the book. This plan avoids a heavy hit on the congregation's anniversary budget. Distribution is handled the same way as above.

Other congregations calculate the unit cost of each book according to the printer's estimate and charge each member family and individual who wants one a few cents more than the cost. This plan is most effective if members who want copies pay for the book before it is printed. That helps to keep the total number of printed copies down to a reasonable number.

Unfortunately, if the total number of preordered books is small, the unit cost of each book goes up substantially. Another difficulty is having enough extra books on hand to sell to members who did not order them but decide they would like to have one after they see it.

The most expensive publication in any printing job is the first one off the press. The more copies that are printed after the first, the lower the cost of each copy. Keep in mind that a congregation's anniversary history can be a valuable resource well after the celebration. Copies should be sent to the local library, the city, county, and state historical societies, and the regional and national judicatory offices and archives of the faith group.

Print enough copies so that the congregation will be able to use them for several years as gifts to new-member families, guest preachers, speakers, teachers, and others who show a special interest in the congregation. Your congregation will be glad it has them.

Adapting Anniversary Planning for Other Events

Anniversaries are the most momentous of congregational celebrations, but they certainly are not the only ones. We already discussed a whole catalog of possible events connected with a congregation's building program in chapter 6. Other special events you might want to give attention in the form of additional publications include the installation of a new pastor or other staff person, the ordination of a member of the congregation, and festival worship services.

Everything that applies to the planning of a congregation's anniversary celebration also applies to every other special occasion. The preparation time is shorter, the number of people who are involved is probably fewer, the publications that are needed most likely are not as complicated, but the elements of planning are essentially the same.

Dedicatory Programs

Since every building project is contracted with a completion date, you know when the dedication will take place and when the printed dedicatory program needs to be available. What should that printed program include? Obvious content includes the order of the dedicatory service, the participants in that service, and the congregation's usual identifying information. Optional additional content includes photos of the new structure, floor plans, the names of the architectural and construction firms and of the chief architect and the construction foreperson, a listing of subcontractors, the names of members of the building committee, and the names of members of the council. Photos of the pastor and other staff appropriate to the occasion and photos of events leading up to the dedication, such as groundbreaking and datestone placement, would help to dress up the design. A brief history of the congregation and the chain of events and decisions leading up to the new construction might also be included.

The budget, of course, dictates how many pages can be used for the printed program, and the number of pages dictates how much material might be included. The key is having people think ahead to decide how useful a printed dedicatory program can be in the ministry of the congregation, and then budgeting and creating accordingly.

Introductory Brochures

Some form of introductory brochure is a standard operating tool for new congregations in areas with growing populations. Most often, it is carried by the pastor and others who are calling on people to invite them into participation in the life of the congregation. The brochures are left with the household as a reminder of the visit and an invitation to worship. Older congregations in established communities could also use similar publications to advantage. What are the attributes that make such documents useful?

Start with format. You want something handy and easy to carry. Two-fold, six-panel pieces work well. If you start with an 8½ by 11 inch page, that gives you a finished brochure in which each panel is 8½ by 3⅝ inches. Start with a 9 by 12 inch piece of paper, and you end up with a 9 by 4 inch folder. The 9 by 4 inch dimension is a little more sophisticated and fits perfectly in a number 10 envelope. The small folder also fits inside a number 10 envelope, but it tends to rattle around in the space a bit more.

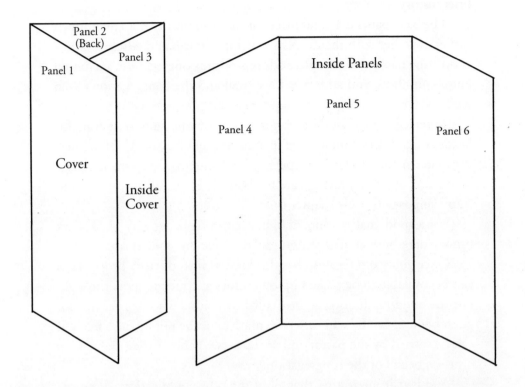

Now think about content. The cover panel identifies your congregation and gives the address. The text could start off with phrases such as: "Introducing," "Welcome to," or "You are invited to visit," followed by the name of the congregation. You might want to include a photograph or line drawing of the worship center.

When you open the brochure, the panel that comes up on the right (the far left panel of the side that includes the cover) is the most difficult to handle because its content works best if it is complete on that page. Think of it as an "inside cover." Content possibilities include a photo and brief biography of the pastor, a brief, bulleted listing of the congregation's theological tenets, or a map of the area showing the location of the building.

The three inside panels could include any of the material above not already used on the opening right-hand panel under the cover. Those inside panels might also carry a description of the congregation's programs of service and ministry, opportunities for education for all ages, possibilities for the use of musical talents in the choir or instrumental groups, special ministries for youth and children, and a brief history.

The back panel is a good place for the community map mentioned earlier, together with the times of worship services and education programs, the name and complete address of the congregation, including phone numbers, and addresses for e-mail and the congregation's Web page.

Typefaces can include a combination of one sans serif font for heads and one serif font for text in a minimum of 11 on 13 pt. (review the material about selecting typefaces in chapter 5). Keep the language of the text objective, taking care to avoid an excess of "we," "us," and "our" language (review chapter 4).

Use a good quality white or light earth-tone paper with black, dark brown, dark blue, or dark burgundy ink. One ink is adequate.

Once your congregation has this kind of introductory brochure, it can be available to be picked up by visitors at strategic spots throughout the building. It also can be mailed to visitors who register in your guest book, it can be sent to representatives of the public media, and it can be carried by the pastor and lay leaders whenever they are making visits on behalf of the congregation.

And isn't it interesting that all of the other publications discussed in this chapter—from anniversary histories to printed dedicatory programs—can be additionally effective when used the same way?

13

Leftovers

Getting the Word Out has laid out a smorgasbord of ideas and recommendations regarding parish publications and public relations and how congregations might improve their ministry both to members and communities by evaluating and revitalizing their communications tools.

But sometimes it is hard to find appropriate places for every dish that is brought to the table, and seldom is a smorgasbord completely consumed. The result? Leftovers. The food in leftovers—particularly after a large festival dinner—is often more tasty the second time around. And leftovers are what chapter 13 is all about.

Colored Papers and Colored Inks

Once again, readability is the key to choosing the right paper. You have worked with objective language and with consistent style and with serif typefaces to make a publication's content as readable as possible (see chapters 4 and 5).

Try not to ruin all that work by deciding that dark purple is a good, liturgical color for the paper used for Advent and Lenten worship service folders, or by using a dark red or green paper for Christmas or other festivals. Print just one copy when you are about to do that, then look at it and give it to a few people around the office with just one criterion in mind: "Can people read it?" or, more to the point, "Can people read it easily?" Stretch the test a bit farther by looking at it in the dimmer light in the sanctuary where people will be reading it at night.

I have seen a few extreme cases where someone wanted to double up the color theme. Not only did they use dark purple paper, but they also printed the text on purple paper with dark purple ink. Readability was hopeless, but at least it was liturgical.

If you have reams of dark colored paper stacked up in your office, turn it into notepads for the pastor and other office staff. Do not use it for any publications for the public.

Stay with white or light-toned paper. If you want to add color, try dark colored inks that have at least four parts black in their composition. Blues, browns, purples, and burgundies work well.

Two other papers are problematical. One is called "confetti," which is a white paper that is imbedded randomly with small flecks of pink, blue, yellow, and several other colors. When those flecks appear under type, they can change the shape of the letter and they affect readability.

Another problematic paper is a rainbow collection of about five pastel colors. Some congregations use the rainbow by making each page of the newsletter a different color. It might be cute, but readers have to adjust to a different test of readability every time they turn the page, which creates another readability problem.

Standard and "Ultra-Standard" Sizes and Formats

The limitations of copying machines in the offices of most congregations restrict publication sizes to those that can be folded out of 8½ by 11 inch or 8½ by 14 inch pages of paper. However, when a congregation goes outside its own office operation for a special publication it sometimes gets talked into producing a booklet that is considerable bigger than those standard sizes.

Be careful here. An oversized publication is usually sophisticated and attracts initial attention easily. But think about what people—or even your own office—will do with it after it has outlived its currency and usefulness. Will it fit in your files, or even on your bookshelves? If not, is the initial flash adequate to overcome its guaranteed shorter usefulness?

The difficulties with unusually sized pieces gets even worse if they have to be mailed. The printing of special-sized envelopes is enormously expensive, particularly for small press runs.

You do not want your pricey publication to have to be folded one more time to fit a standard envelope. An extra fold that was not originally designed to be part of a publication destroys its original effect. You also do not want your publication to fit too loosely in an envelope that is the next size up and a disproportionate shape.

Think about use, length of life, and distribution before you put an important and expensive publication on the press and make sure the design fits a standard envelope. Your printer can show you what envelopes are available, and tell you the cost of the envelopes and the additional costs of having them imprinted with your congregation's logo and return address.

Developing Your Congregation's Logo

Logos are significant marks of a congregation's identity. First, a distinction: most congregations have an official seal. It might show up on stationery, and it might be on an embossing tool that is someplace in the pastor's office. It is not used often, nor should it be. It needs to be restricted for use only on official documents. But a seal is not a logo.

A congregation's logo is a symbol that is generally less formal and can be used on stationery, newsletters, worship service guides, mugs, cookbooks, and all other publications, as well as your Web site, advertising, and the outdoor identity sign. It can even be made a part of a congregation's indoor signage that identifies rooms and offices.

Good logos, after they have been introduced, take on lives of their own. Just like the logos of insurance companies and other businesses, the logo of a congregation becomes an acknowledged and recognizable mark of identity.

The first thing that marks a good logo is simplicity—logos cannot be cluttered. Words are seldom incorporated into the design unless the word itself is given a bit of decoration and made to stand alone as a company's logo. It is also important to remember that a bit of ambiguity can be useful in broadening the potential meaning of the symbolism.

Congregations often use stylized crosses, forms of flame (for the spirit), lambs (referring to the Lamb of God), eagles and lions (references to writers of the Gospels), open books, and sacramental symbols among many other elements that reflect the mission and life of the faith group. Synagogues frequently use six-pointed stars of David and seven-candled menorah in their symbolism.

It is usually best for a congregation to employ a professional graphic designer when it begins its search for a logo. If a designer happens to be a member of the congregation, this is a bonus, but the person should still be paid for his work (see chapter 12). If the designer wants to return his fee as a gift to the congregation, that's fine, but he should still be paid.

First, the public relations committee should discuss the idea of a special logo thoroughly. What do members of the committee want to convey about the congregation's life and ministry? What symbols do they think might be most dramatic and communicative?

Then, once the committee reaches consensus, either the entire committee or a selected representative should meet with a designer to talk about what the congregation wants its logo to convey. Discuss the congregation's background, traditions, and ministry. Also be plain about the decision process once initial sketches are in hand. And, of course, settle on the designer's fee.

The designer should prepare three to five rough sketches of logo ideas. Once those are in hand, pass them around to the congregation's staff and members of the council to see if any of the ideas rise to the top as the preponderant choice. If that does not happen, keep a record of which parts of the symbolism involved seem to resonate better than others.

Take the most popular ideas back to the designer and ask for a new set of drawings that incorporate the most popular and communicative ideas. Now you might have to go through the original choosing process all over again, but eventually one sketch will move to the forefront as the favorite. Be patient and take your time. Once you make the final decision on the choice of your logo, it should be expected to serve the congregation as a significant tool of communication for up to a decade or more.

There are reasons why you do not want to change logos often. First, the development of a logo can be relatively expensive. Second, the logo is an integral part of your congregation's visual identity, and you want that identity to be sustained.

When the designer delivers the finished art, he should also offer a usage guide with suggestions about how the logo should and should not be used. The guide will recommend the typeface to be used with the logo when adding the name and address of the congregation. It will also show the preferred positioning of the logo on the page for various kinds of layouts, size, and spacing guidelines. Finally, the guide will indicate preferred ink colors when used in publications printed in more than one color. Now your congregation has a graphic identity.

Once the logo and graphic identity are in hand, introduce them to the congregation with an article in the periodic newsletter. Describe the logo's symbolism and the ways in which it tells the story of the congregation. Announce ground rules for where and how it can be used, and discourage integration of the congregation's logo into other organizational logos that might be in use. Let people know who will monitor and control its use.

Then enjoy this significant addition to your accumulation of communication resources.

Enlivening the Congregation's Stationery

The first impression made by a congregation's stationery is significant. The style of the typography, the use of a logo, the presentation of identifying information, and the quality of paper all work together in a statement of who and what the congregation is before the recipient even reads the letter it carries.

Even the choice of paper can affect that first impression. Is it plain white, multipurpose, 20-pound paper out of the supply used for the copying machine, with plain white, number 10 envelopes on which the return address has been rubber stamped?

No question about the economy of that practice, but it might be a situation of "penny wise and pound foolish." The first impression is either one of a congregation that must be "just getting by" or, worse, of one that really does not care what imprint it might be leaving on the community where it ministers.

A visit to your local printer can acquaint you with a variety of attractive papers, some with a touch of texture, some in pleasant earthtone colors, all with matching envelopes, and many that are still economical.

If a graphic artist has just designed a logo for the congregation, expand the assignment to include suggestions for stationery that incorporates that logo and uses typefaces compatible with the logo in a deep, vibrant color that helps to communicate the life and vitality of your congregation. It is important. Your congregation's stationery does make an important impression.

At minimum, the information on the letterhead includes the name of the congregation, its address, phone number, the name of the pastor, and the e-mail and Web addresses, all in a typeface compatible with the congregation's publications. The font is a contemporary serif face, mostly cap and lowercase, gradated in sizes depending on the logical significance of the information, with the smallest size being no less than 9 pt. It is not in a typeface such as Old English.

Even with today's propensity for communication through e-mail, congregations still need attractive, communicative stationery for their more formal contacts. Your congregation's stationery does make a difference. Give it serious attention.

All about Advertising

One of the places where your logo can be used effectively is in paid advertising in the public media.

Many congregations join with others in the weeks before Christmas, Easter, and the holidays of other faith groups to buy newspaper ads that announce the times of their worship services and invite the public to come. Usually, this is not very expensive advertising, but it is also not very effective. Often, it is a matter of self-protection since congregation's have learned they can be conspicuous by their absence.

Much better is a planned campaign of ads run at least once a month that raise questions about issues of faith and life and reminds readers that the congregation is there to help them find answers to those questions. If an advertising director of a public relations firm happens to be a member of your congregation, perhaps that person can be enlisted to help with such a campaign. It is not easy to write advertising copy that simplifies issues of faith and asks questions that trigger the response of attendance at a worship service.

Some faith groups have spent hundreds of thousands of dollars on the research and development of a series of ads that have been successful in doing just that. Contact your denomination to find out if it has such a program, and if the ads it developed are available for use by individual congregations. If so, all you have to do is contact the appropriate newspapers, add the imprint of your congregation, set up a schedule of placement, and pay for the space.

Since advertising is most effective when it is repetitive, the denominations that have developed print ads have often completed the package by producing complementary ads for radio and television. If your congregation can budget sponsorship of the whole print, radio, and TV package in your community, even for only a few months each year, it can have a tremendously positive impact, not only for your congregation but also for the faith group at large.

If your congregation thinks such a broad and extended advertising program is too expensive, perhaps it can band together with others in the area in the same denomination and sponsor an ad campaign together.

Broadcasting Worship Services

While we are talking about electronic media, many congregations—particularly in small towns—broadcast their worship service live every Sunday on the local radio station. Others go a step further and videotape each service for broadcast later on a local community TV channel. The specific advertising value of such practices is small, but they cost relatively little. Such broadcasts serve well the members of the congregation who are hospitalized and homebound, but announcements of the specific times of the broadcasts need to be included regularly in the parish newsletter.

Taking Advantage of Billboards

Two other public advertising vehicles need to be mentioned. The first is billboards. Congregations often overlook the billboard opportunity because they think automatically that such advertising is too expensive. Billboard companies never like to see empty space or out-of-date content on the boards they own that dot the urban and rural landscapes.

Rather than leave their boards either empty or in a state of becoming an eyesore, they would rather fill them with something informative. Watch the billboards in your congregation's neighborhood. When one becomes out of date and unchanged for several weeks, go to the billboard company, emphasize your nonprofit status, and ask if that board space might be used to advertise your congregation's worship services or some other part of your program.

It is probable that the company will be glad to fill the board with your congregation's ad, and all your congregation has to pay is the printing cost for the paper that carries your message. The billboard company might even help you design your ad. If you have been using a media advertising package from your denomination, it probably includes ideas for billboard advertising. Be aware, however, that if the billboard company finds a buyer for that space, it is likely your ad will disappear in favor of one that is paying full price.

A second advertising idea on a smaller scale but with a potentially bigger impact for urban and suburban congregations is to contact the local bus company about advertising placards that fit into the space above the windows around the interior perimeter of the bus. You might be surprised about how reasonable the rates will be for your nonprofit organization.

Newsletter Advertising

One completely different kind of advertising needs attention. Some congregations—the practice seems to be more prevalent in some denominations than others—include a page of ads in each newsletter. The ads are usually a little smaller than a business card and include business card information. The advertisers are generally, but not exclusively, members of the congregation.

The idea is to give members a list of businesses owned by members and businesses around the neighborhood of the place of worship that can be patronized by members. The ads, which usually cost only a few dollars each, offset a relatively small portion of the costs of printing and distributing the newsletter.

This practice has a few problems. First, the cost of the newsletter (as well as other publications) is handled best when paid out of the congregation's annual budget just like all of the other elements of ongoing ministry. That way, all members have more of a sense of full participation in all of the aspects of the congregation's life. Tapping members for small and cheap monthly ads in the newsletter has a tendency to downgrade the publication's significance and effectiveness because it seems the congregation's leadership does not think this vital communications vehicle is important enough to stand on its own.

Second, the minimal amounts requested from individuals and businesses to run the ads too often have the possibility of setting the stage for minimal stewardship. It is better for everyone to participate equally in the congregation's communications program through more substantial gifts that support its total ministry. Full budgeting of the communications program changes the idea of ownership (and stewardship) from the few who advertise to the whole congregation whose gifts support the full mission of faith.

If the idea is to promote use of members' businesses by other members, set aside a bulletin board on which everyone can post their business card for free. Members can then check that bulletin board whenever they are looking for any kind of worker or vendor.

If some are concerned that only the 30 percent of the membership who come to worship see the board, publish the list of members' businesses free in the newsletter a couple of times a year.

Caring for the Congregation's Campus

A congregation's buildings and their surrounding grounds form a public campus that needs continuing attention. Let's start with the exterior identification signs and bulletin boards. Some are woefully archaic; they were set up a half a century ago and look it. Even the name of the congregation is too small to be read easily, particularly since it is in a long-ago antiquated Old English (or maybe its old European) typeface.

If the outdoor bulletin board has a place for updating the date, the liturgical day, and the sermon theme or other saying, it is frequently out of date. Furthermore, the type is too small to be read by anyone other than pedestrians strolling by.

What is needed is a contemporary replacement compatible with the building's architecture. The congregation's logo should be prominent, and the name of the congregation needs to be in a modern typeface that is easily readable by the driver of a car going by at 30 miles per hour. Readable is at least eight inches high, and maybe more, depending on how far away it is from the road.

The sign should also include the street address, phone number, and Web site in letters at least half as high as the name of the congregation. A section for movable type might be useful to announce the coming Sunday's sermon theme or a supposedly clever saying. However, the sayings have become a bit of an anachronism. Sometimes, the sayings are far afield from communicating the congregation's mission. Occasionally, they would be better left unposted.

Whatever the messages, outdoor signs should also be lighted, with automatic timers turning the board on at dusk and off at dawn, or if you want to save a bit of electricity, at midnight.

While you are outside, check the parking lot. If it includes light poles, could they be used to hold banners on special Sundays? Multi-colored banners that include the logo and proclaim "Alleluia," "Glory," "Praise to the Lord," "He Is Risen," or "Peace to All" add a festive note to the day before the people even enter the place of worship. Is the parking lot lined, and does it include curbs to help people park their cars most efficiently?

Does the congregation have one or more designated gardeners, either paid or volunteer, who make sure at least once a month that flower beds are planted and watered and that foundation plantings are trimmed and weeded? A few flowers—annuals and perennials—can do wonders to turn a commonplace landscape into a showplace.

For northern climes, when gardens are frozen and covered with snow, are arrangements made to make sure the parking lot is plowed and sidewalks are shoveled and sanded well before people start arriving for meetings or worship services?

Making the Building a Place of Welcome

Inside the building, do signs give clear directions to offices, restrooms, classrooms, and lounges? Have bulletin boards in the hallways been cleaned of outdated posters and announcements? Is someone responsible to check and change the bulletin boards at least every two weeks so that information is presented attractively?

At the entrances to the sanctuary, do volunteers greet and welcome everyone? Do ushers make sure every worshiper receives a worship service guide? Do banners on the sanctuary walls announce the season or the theme for that day's worship service?

Members often talk about their faith home; therefore, it is important that the congregation's building always offers a friendly face, both inside and out. This cannot be separated from the congregation's mission and ministry. Never forget that the building and the surrounding grounds also communicate and are, in themselves, witnesses.

This is how it should be with every form of communication your congregation uses to reach its members, its prospects, the media, and everyone else.

Conclusion

Concerns about parish publications and public relations reflected in *Getting the Word Out* have come back time and time again to the theological benchmarks of mission and ministry, life and worship, stewardship and evangelism, education and leadership. All of those vital signs of faith and service are tied together by effective communication.

Analyzing the newsletter's competition, discovering the purpose of a parish publications program, and taking a closer look at a congregation's audiences and demographics are all preliminary necessities to the creation of effective communications tools that make a difference.

Being aware of the essential factors of assured readability of language and format is an ever-present challenge that demands alert response. Picking readable fonts, placing them in readable line lengths, maintaining a consistent style, and keeping the language objective and aimed at the future are all tasks that need continuing attention.

Broadening the content of newsletters and worship service guides and making them work together as a team instills new life and excitement in the communications package you create to enhance a congregation's ministry.

Bolstering editorial responsibility with editorial authority, and organizing an active public relations committee in the congregation relieves pastors of such concerns and makes better use of the lay talent that is eager to serve. Working with media for mutual benefits and creating a crisis plan that you hope you never have to use gives the congregation's leadership confidence as well as visibility.

Using photography effectively and keeping clip art under control helps to make your parish publications more competitive as well as communicative. Opening up to the possibilities of electronic communication through e-mail and the Web broadens the congregation's outreach.

Taking advantage of every opportunity to highlight and celebrate special events adds enthusiasm to the congregation's life and mission.

Congregational communication can be compared to a web that touches, connects, and even sensitizes all the elements of congregational ministry. Make it the best that it can be. And while you're at it, enjoy the challenge.

Appendix A

Self-Study and Analysis

A guide for a communications, publications, or public relations audit done by the congregation for itself.

I. Who is the congregation's audience? (See chapter 3.)

Size of Congregation? _____

Baptized? _____

Confirmed? _____

Giving Units? _____

Demographics by age (percentage of males/females in each age group in congregation):

0–12 _____/_____%

13–19 _____/_____%

20–29 _____/_____%

30–39 _____/_____%

40–49 _____/_____%

50–59 _____/_____%

60–69 _____/_____%

70–80 _____/_____%

80+ _____/_____%

Describing and numbering by categories (See chapter 2.):

Core _____

Muscle _____

Inactives _____

Hospitalized _____

Seasonal Movers _____

Prospects? _____

Media/Exchanges _____

Men _____

Women _____

Youth _____

Married _____

Both spouses work _____

Single _____

Divorced _____

Widowed _____

II. Develop statements of mission / purpose for publications / public relations
   A. General (See chapter 2.)

_____

_____

_____

_____

   B. Newsletters (See chapters 2, 4, 5, 6.)

_____

_____

_____

_____

_____

_____

_____

C. Worship Service Folders (See chapters 2, 4, 5, 7.)

_____

_____

_____

_____

_____

_____

_____

D. Other (See chapters 2, 4, 5, 12.)

_____

_____

_____

_____

III. Who is the Congregation's Publications Competition? (See chapter 1.)

_____

_____

_____

_____

_____

_____

IV. Content Review (See chapter 6 and chapter 7.)

Newsletter Content Now   **Newsletter Content Potential**

_____   _____

_____   _____

_____   _____

_____   _____

_____   _____

_____   _____

_____   _____

_____   _____

_____   _____

_____   _____

_____   _____

_____   _____

_____   _____

_____   _____

_____   _____

_____   _____

_____   _____

_____   _____

Service Guide Content Now   **Service Guide Content Potential**

_____   _____

_____   _____

_____   _____

_____   _____

_____   _____

_____   _____

_____   _____

_____   _____

_____   _____

_____   _____

_____   _____

_____   _____

_____   _____

_____   _____
_____   _____
_____   _____
_____   _____
_____   _____
_____   _____
_____   _____

V. Organizational Considerations (See chapter 8.)
   (For discussion and possible implementation.)
   A. The question of the editor's responsibility / authority
   B. Organization solutions
      1. Regular conferences with pastor(s) / appropriate staff / members
         a. e-mail communication
         b. moving material on discs
      2. Public relations committee (three to seven people)
         a. Editor (paid or volunteer)
         b. Communications professionals/interested persons from church
         c. Postal employee
         d. Meets once a month soon after newsletter mailed
            1) Critiques previous month's publications
            2) Provides content ideas for coming issues
            3) Suggests format / design changes

VI. Self-critique of recent publications and other communications efforts.
    (To be filled out by the publications editor and members of the public relations committee.)

    A. Weekly worship service folders (See chapters 4–7.)

_____
_____
_____
_____
_____

B. Special worship service folders (See chapters 4–7.)

_____

_____

_____

_____

_____

_____

C. Periodic Newsletter (See chapters 4–7.)

_____

_____

_____

_____

_____

_____

_____

_____

_____

D. Special publications by name (See chapters 4–7, 12.)

_____: _____

_____

_____

_____: _____

_____

_____

_____: _____

_____

_____

E. Web page (See chapter 11.)

_____

_____

_____

_____

_____

F. E-mail communication (See chapter 11.)

_____

_____

_____

G. Interior bulletin boards (See chapter 13.)

_____

_____

_____

H. Exterior bulletin boards (See chapter 13.)

_____

_____

_____

I. Interior signage (See chapter 13.)

_____

_____

_____

Appendix B

Elements of Publication Style

A Beginning Style Sheet

The following suggestions are based on the *Associated Press Stylebook and Libel Manual* (Cambridge, Mass.: Perseus Publishing, 2002). A more formal style can be patterned after *The Chicago Manual of Style*, 15th ed. (Chicago and London: University of Chicago Press, 2003). Both books should be available in your local bookstore or can be purchased on the Internet. See chapter 4 for suggestions on developing your own consistent style sheet for your own congregation.

Abbreviations

Months—abbreviate all months of more than four letters unless they are used without a date.

Days—abbreviate days only if they are used in conjunction with dates.

Time—use lower case letters with periods (a.m. or p.m.); never use "o'clock," and never use "evening and p.m." or "morning and a.m." in the same sentence.

States—abbreviate all states with more than five letters. Standard forms include: Minn., Iowa, Ill., S.D., N.D., Wis., Nebr., Penn., Ind., Mich., Ohio, Ariz., Fla., and so forth. (Two-letter zip code abbreviations can be used, but they are aesthetically unattractive.)

Dates—ordinal designations such as st, nd, rd, th are not necessary and should not be used.

Years—do not designate the year in a current date unless leaving it out might confuse the reader

Capitalization

- Capitalize all **proper names** (St. John's Lutheran Church).
- Do not capitalize **generic synonyms** (the congregation).

- Capitalize the initial letter of each word in **titles** of hymns, sermons, books, and so forth, except prepositions and articles.
- Capitalize the initial letter of each word in Newsletter Headlines except prepositions and articles.
- When in doubt, start the word with a lowercase letter.

Names and Titles

- The first time a **person's name** is used in a story, it should include first and last names (and possibly middle initial).
- **Subsequent references** to the same person should use either the first name or the last, but not both. Use of last name only is preferable, but consistency is most important.
- The use of **titles** is not necessary and can be omitted.
- If **titles** are used, they should be abbreviated.
- Standard forms are: Mr., Ms., Mrs., Dr., Pr., the Rev. (Pr. has become a recognized abbreviation for pastor in some faith groups. Reverend is not a noun, but an adjective.)
- When a person is **identified** with a description ahead of the name, the descriptive word should be capitalized (Council President Jane Jones).
- When a **description** is used after a name, it should be in lowercase and separated with commas (Jane Jones, council president).
- The first time a **proper noun** is used, it should be spelled out and followed by the appropriate acronym in parenthesis: Evangelical Lutheran Church in America (ELCA).
- **Subsequent usage** of the name should be only the acronym without parentheses, or a synonym (the church).

Punctuation

- Do not use a comma before the conjunction preceding the last item in a series.
- Do not use multiple exclamation points or question marks.
- Separate dates and years with a comma and use a comma after the year.
- Do not use commas between a month and year if no date is included.

Appendix C: Demonstrations in Readability

Note how readability increases as lines are shortened, size of type is increased, and style of type shifts from sans serif (Helvetica) to a serif (Times New Roman) typeface.

Times New Roman 12 pt. on 14 pt.

Readability is affected both by content and typography.

If the content is not substantive, objective, clear, concise, accurate and to the point, readability suffers. Sentences should be short, active and direct. They should avoid cliches and overuse of adverbs and adjectives.

Readability suffers when typography does not help the reader through the material, and the page is cluttered, gives the impression of being unorganized and is overworked with too many different typefaces.

The most readable type faces are regular, light face, serif (Roman) rather than sans serif (block letter) styles.

The optimum line length is one and one-half lower case alphabets (39 letters and spaces). Line lengths of more than two alphabets (52 letters and spaces) or less than one alphabet (26 letters and spaces) decrease readability dramatically.

Emphases such as ALL CAPS, CAPS AND SMALL CAPS, **boldface**, *italic*, and <u>underline</u> decrease readability and should never be used in large blocks. Never use more than one typographical emphasis at one time on any word or group of words.

Helvetica 10 pt. on 12 pt.

Readability is affected both by content and typography.

If the content is not substantive, objective, clear, concise, accurate and to the point, readability suffers. Sentences should be short, active and direct. They should avoid cliches and overuse of adverbs and adjectives.

Readability suffers when typography does not help the reader through the material, and the page is cluttered, gives the impression of being unorganized and is overworked with too many different typefaces.

The most readable type faces are regular, light face, serif (Roman) rather than sans serif (block letter) styles.

The optimum line length is one and one-half lower case alphabets (39 letters and spaces). Line lengths of more than two alphabets (52 letters and spaces) or less than one alphabet (26 letters and spaces) decrease readability dramatically.

Emphases such as ALL CAPS, CAPS AND SMALL CAPS, **boldface**, *italic*, and <u>underline</u> decrease readability and should never be used in large blocks. Never use more than one typographical emphasis at one time on any word or group of words.

Times New Roman 11 pt. on 13 pt.

Readability is affected both by content and typography.

If the content is not substantive, objective, clear, concise, accurate and to the point, readability suffers. Sentences should be short, active and direct. They should avoid cliches and overuse of adverbs and adjectives.

Readability suffers when typography does not help the reader through the material, and the page is cluttered, gives the impression of being unorganized and is overworked with too many different typefaces.

The most readable type faces are regular, light face, serif (Roman) rather than sans serif (block letter) styles.

The optimum line length is one and one-half lower case alphabets (39 letters and spaces). Line lengths of more than two alphabets (52 letters and spaces) or less than one alphabet (26 letters and spaces) decrease readability dramatically.

Emphases such as ALL CAPS, CAPS AND SMALL CAPS, **boldface**, *italic*, and <u>underline</u> decrease readability and should never be used in large blocks. Never use more than one typographical emphasis at one time on any word or group of words.

Times New Roman 10 pt. on 12 pt.

Readability is affected both by content and typography.

If the content is not substantive, objective, clear, concise, accurate and to the point, readability suffers. Sentences should be short, active and direct. They should avoid cliches and overuse of adverbs and adjectives.

Readability suffers when typography does not help the reader through the material, and the page is cluttered, gives the impression of being unorganized and is overworked with too many different typefaces.

The most readable type faces are regular, light face, serif (Roman) rather than sans serif (block letter) styles.

The optimum line length is one and one-half lower case alphabets (39 letters and spaces). Line lengths of more than two alphabets (52 letters and spaces) or less than one alphabet (26 letters and spaces) decrease readability dramatically.

Emphases such as ALL CAPS, CAPS AND SMALL CAPS, **boldface**, *italic*, and <u>underline</u> decrease readability and should never be used in large blocks. Never use more than one typographical emphasis at one time on any word or group of words.

Helvetica 9 pt. on 11 pt.

*Note the substantial differences below in the sizes of type,
the amount of space used, and the readability*

Readability is affected both by content and typography.

If the content is not substantive, objective, clear, concise, accurate and to the point, readability suffers. Sentences should be short, active and direct. They should avoid cliches and overuse of adverbs and adjectives.

Readability suffers when typography does not help the reader through the material, and the page is cluttered, gives the impression of being unorganized and is overworked with too many different typefaces.

The most readable type faces are regular, light face, serif (Roman) rather than sans serif (block letter) styles.

The optimum line length is one and one-half lower case alphabets (39 letters and spaces). Line lengths of more than two alphabets (52

Helvetica 10 pt. on 12 pt.

Readability is affected both by content and typography.

If the content is not substantive, objective, clear, concise, accurate and to the point, readability suffers. Sentences should be short, active and direct. They should avoid cliches and overuse of adverbs and adjectives.

Readability suffers when typography does not help the reader through the material, and the page is cluttered, gives the impression of being unorganized and is overworked with too many different typefaces.

The most readable type faces are regular, light face, serif (Roman) rather than sans serif (block letter) styles.

The optimum line length is one

Helvetica 11 pt. on 13 pt.

Readability is affected both by content and typography.

If the content is not substantive, objective, clear, concise, accurate and to the point, readability suffers. Sentences should be short, active and direct. They should avoid cliches and overuse of adverbs and adjectives.

Readability suffers when typography does not help the reader through the material, and the page is cluttered, gives the impression of being unorganized and is overworked with too many different typefaces.

The most readable type

Helvetica 12 pt. on 14 pt.

Readability is affected both by content and typography.

If the content is not substantive, objective, clear, concise, accurate and to the point, readability suffers. Sentences should be short, active and direct. They should avoid cliches and overuse of adverbs and adjectives.

Readability suffers when typography does not help the reader through the material, and the page is cluttered, gives the impression of being unorganized and is overworked with too many different typefaces.

The most readable type faces are regular, light face, serif (Roman) rather than sans serif (block letter) styles.

The optimum line length is one and one-half lower case alphabets (39 letters and spaces). Line lengths of more than two alphabets (52 letters and spaces) or less than one alphabet (26 letters and spaces decrease

Times New Roman 10 pt. on 12 pt.

Readability is affected both by content and typography.

If the content is not substantive, objective, clear, concise, accurate and to the point, readability suffers. Sentences should be short, active and direct. They should avoid cliches and overuse of adverbs and adjectives.

Readability suffers when typography does not help the reader through the material, and the page is cluttered, gives the impression of being unorganized and is overworked with too many different typefaces.

The most readable type faces are regular, light face, serif (Roman) rather than sans serif (block letter) styles.

The optimum line length is one and one-half lower case alphabets (39 letters and spaces). Line lengths

Times New Roman 11 pt. on 13 pt.

Readability is affected both by content and typography.

If the content is not substantive, objective, clear, concise, accurate and to the point, readability suffers. Sentences should be short, active and direct. They should avoid cliches and overuse of adverbs and adjectives.

Readability suffers when typography does not help the reader through the material, and the page is cluttered, gives the impression of being unorganized and is overworked with too many different typefaces.

The most readable type faces are regular, light face, serif (Roman) rather than sans serif (block letter) styles.

Times New Roman 12 pt. on 14 pt.

Emphases such as ALL CAPS, CAPS AND SMALL CAPS, **boldface**, *italic*, underline, and reverse decrease readability and should never be used in large blocks. Never use more than one typographical emphasis at one time on any word or group of words

---

Readability is affected both by content and typography.

IF THE CONTENT IS NOT SUBSTANTIVE, OBJECTIVE, CLEAR, CONCISE, ACCURATE AND TO THE POINT, READABILITY SUFFERS. SENTENCES SHOULD BE SHORT, ACTIVE AND DIRECT. THEY SHOULD AVOID CLICHES AND OVERUSE OF ADVERBS AND ADJECTIVES.

Readability suffers when typography does not help the reader through the material, and the page is cluttered, gives the impression of being unorganized and is overworked with too many different typefaces.

The most readable type faces are *regular, light face, serif (Roman) rather than sans serif*

Helvetica 10 pt. on 12 pt.

Readability is affected both by content and typography.

IF THE CONTENT IS NOT SUBSTANTIVE, OBJECTIVE, CLEAR, CONCISE, ACCU-RATE AND TO THE POINT, READABILITY SUFFERS. SEN-TENCES SHOULD BE SHORT, ACTIVE AND DIRECT. THEY SHOULD AVOID CLICHES AND OVERUSE OF ADVERBS

Readability suffers when typography does not help the reader through the material, and the page is cluttered, gives the impression of being unor-ganized and is overworked with too many different

Helvetica 11 pt. on 13 pt.

Readability is affected both by content and typography.

IF THE CONTENT IS NOT SUBSTANTIVE, OBJECTIVE, CLEAR, CONCISE, ACCURATE AND TO THE POINT, READABILITY SUFFERS. SENTENCES SHOULD BE SHORT, ACTIVE AND DIRECT. THEY SHOULD AVOID CLICHES AND OVERUSE OF ADVERBS AND ADJECTIVES.

Readability suffers when typography does not help the reader through the material, and the page is cluttered, gives the impression of being unorganized and is over-worked with too many differ-ent typefaces.

Helvetica 12 pt. on 14 pt.

Readability is affected both by content and typography.

IF THE CONTENT IS NOT SUBSTANTIVE, OBJECTIVE, CLEAR, CONCISE, ACCURATE AND TO THE POINT, READABILITY SUFFERS. SENTENCES SHOULD BE SHORT, ACTIVE AND DIRECT. THEY SHOULD AVOID CLICHES AND OVERUSE OF ADVERBS AND ADJECTIVES.

Readability suffers when typography does not help the reader through the material, and the page is cluttered, gives the impression of being unorganized and is overworked with too many different typefaces.

The most readable type faces are regular, light face, serif (Roman) rather than sans serif (block letter) styles.

Times New Roman 10 pt. on 12 pt.

Readability is affected both by content and typography.

If the content is not substantive, objective, clear, concise, accurate and to the point, readability suffers. Sentences should be short, active and direct. They should avoid cliches and overuse of adverbs and adjectives.

Readability suffers when typography does not help the reader through the material, and the page is cluttered, gives the impression of being unorganized and is overworked with too many different typefaces.

The most readable type faces are regular, light face, serif (Roman) rather than sans serif (block letter) styles.

The optimum line length is one and one-half lower case alphabets

Times New Roman 11 pt. on 13 pt.

Readability is affected both by content and typography.

IF THE CONTENT IS NOT SUBSTANTIVE, OBJECTIVE, CLEAR, CONCISE, ACCURATE AND TO THE POINT, READABILITY SUFFERS. SENTENCES SHOULD BE SHORT, ACTIVE AND DIRECT. THEY SHOULD AVOID CLICHES AND OVERUSE OF ADVERBS AND ADJECTIVES.

Readability suffers when typography does not help the reader through the material, and the page is cluttered, gives the impression of being unorganized and

Times New Roman 12 pt. on 14 pt.

Boxes, screens, call outs, and drop caps create their own possibilities of emphasis and variety — together with potential problems

Readability suffers when typography does not help the reader through the material, and the page is cluttered, gives the impression of being unorganized and is overworked with too many different typefaces.

Box too tight.
Text needs room to "breath."

Readability suffers when typography does not help the reader through the material, and the page is cluttered, gives the impression of being unorganized and is overworked with too many

Box about right.
Note space between text and lines.

Readability suffers when typography does not help the reader through the material, and the page is cluttered, gives the impression of being unorganized and is overworked with too many

Screen (20%) calls more attention to material. Harder to read.

Readability is affected both by content and typography. If the content is not substantive, objective, clear, concise, accurate and to the point, readability suffers. Sentences should be short, active and direct. They should avoid cliches and overuse of adverbs and adjectives.

Poor typography often causes poor readability

Readability suffers when typography does not help the reader through the material, and the page is cluttered, gives the impression of being unorganized and is overworked with too many different typefaces.

Readability is affected both by content and typography. If the content is not substantive, objective, clear, concise, accurate and to the point, readability suffers.

Sentences should be short, active and direct.

They should avoid cliches and overuse of adverbs and adjectives.

Poor typography often causes poor readability

Readability suffers when typography does not help the reader through the material, and the page is cluttered, gives the impression of being unorganized and is

Type (above and right): 11 on 13 pt. Times New Roman
Drop Cap: 48 pt. Helvetica Bold in three lines; Call out: 12 on 14 pt. Times New Roman bold
with 4 pt. solid rules top and bottom.

Readability Linked to Format

Readability is affected both by content and typography.

If the content is not substantive, objective, clear, concise, accurate and to the point, readability suffers. Sentences should be short, active and direct. They should avoid cliches and overuse of adverbs and adjectives.

Readability suffers when typography does not help the reader through the material, and the page is cluttered, gives the impression of being unorganized and is overworked with too

Head: 14 on 16 pt. Helvetica with 4 pts. space between head
and text.
Text: 11 on 13 pt. Times New Roman.
Drop cap: 31 pt. bold Times New Roman.
Box: solid 2 pt with round corners

Readability suffers when typography does not help the reader through the material, and the page is cluttered, gives the impression of being unorganized and is overworked with too many different typefaces.

Type: 10 on 12 Times New Roman, reversed;
Box: solid 2 pt. line; Fill: 50 percent screen;
Drop cap, 28.5. pt. Times New Roman

Production Note:
Text was written in Word 97 and formatting was done in QuarkXPress 4.1

Appendix D

Type Specimens List

All the typefaces shown are available in the collection of fonts included in the Microsoft Word 97 application for Windows. All type is set 12 pt. on a 15 pt. line. Note the small percentage of fonts in both serif and sans serif styles that are easily read. The most readable and usable serif faces are noted with a * after the font name. The most readable and usable sans serif faces are marked with ** after the font name. Avoid using any of the remaining fonts in your parish publications.

Abadi MT Condensed Light

Agaramond *

Agaramond Bold *

Alleycat ICG

ANTIQUE

Arial **

Arial Black **

Arial Narrow **

Arial Narrow Special G1 **

Arial Special G1 **

Bavand

BAZOOKA

Bernhard Modern Roman *

Bernhard Modern BT *

Block

Boca Raton ICG

Boca Raton ICG Solid

Book Antiqua

Bookman Old Style *

Boulder

Broadview

CAESAR

Calisto MT *

Calligrapher

Century Gothic

Century Schoolbook *

Cezanne

Chaucer

Chicago ICG Cuatro

Christie

Comic Sans MS

Continuum Bold **

Continuum Light **

Continuum Medium **

COPPERPLATE GOTHIC
BOLD

COPPERPLATE GOTHIC LIGHT
COPPERPLATE 31 AB
COPPERPLATE 33 BC
CORNERSTONE
Cotillion
Courier
Courier New
CRATE
Cuckoo
Curlz MT
DECOTURA ICG
DECOTURA ICG INLINE
Denmark
Diner
Diploma
Elephant
EMERALD ISLE
ENGRAVERS MT
Eras Bold ITC **
Eras Demi ITC **
Eras Light ITC **
Eras Medium ITC **
Erode
FAJITA ICG MILD
FAJITA ICG PICANTE
FELIX TITLING
Fifth Avenue
FILLMORE
Fitzerald
Fixedsys
Forte
Franciscan
Franklin Gothic Book **

Franklin Gothic Condensed **
Franklin Gothic Demi **
Franklin Gothic Demi Condensed **
Franklin Gothic Medium **
Franklin Gothic Medium
    Condensed **
Franklin Gothic No. 2 **
French Script MT
Garamond *
Garamond Book Condensed *
Garamond Light Condensed *
GASLIGHT
Georgia
Gill Sans MT
Gill Sans MT Condensed
Gill Sans MT Extra Condensed Bold
Gill Sans Ultra Bold
Gill Sans Ultra Bold Condensed
Gloucester MT Extra Condensed
Goudy *
Goudy Old Style *
Haettenschweiler
Heather
Helv **
Helvetica **
Herald
Impact
Imprint MT Shadow
Intrepid
Intrepid Extrabold
Invitation
ITC Officina Sans Book
ITC Officina Serif Book
Janis

Jester
Julius
Librarian
Litterbox ICG
Long Island
Lucinda Console
Lucinda Handwriting
Lucinda Sans **
Lucinda Sans Typewriter **
Lucinda Sans Unicode **
Maiandra GD
Mariah
Market
MATISSE ITC
METRO
Moderne
Myriad Roman
News Gothic MT **
NewZurica
Nuptial Script
OCR A Extended
OCR B MT
Old Century
Patsley ICG 01
Patsley ICG 01 Alt
Patsley ICG 02
Patsley ICG 02 Alt
Palace Script MT
Palatia *
Paper Punch
PAPERCLIP
Paramount *
Park Avenue

Partridge
Patrick
Pegasus
Percival
Perpetua *
PERPETUA TITLING MT
Pickwick
Poster
Prestige Elite
Pythagoras
Quick Type **
Quick Type Condensed **
Quick Type II **
Quick Type II Condensed **
Quick Type II Mono **
Quill
Rage Italic
ROCKSTONE
Rockwell
Rockwell Condensed
Rockwell Extra Bold
Roman
Saloon
Saturday Sans ICG
Sceptre
Scratch
SCRiBBLE
Script MT Bold
Sherwood
Signature
SIGNBOARD
Small Fonts
Snell Bd BT

Sniff

Socket

StageCoach

STANDOUT

Stars & Stripes

STEAMER

STENCIL

Stewardson

Stonehenge

Storybook

Stylus

Submarine

Subway

Συμβολ (Symbol)

System **

Tabitha

Tahoma

Tekton

Teletype

Tempus Sans ITC

Terminal

Times *

Times New Roman *

Times New Roman Condensed *

Times New Roman Special GI *

TRAJAN

TRANSISTOR

Treasure

TRISTAN

Tubular

Tw Cen MT

Tw Cen MT Condensed

Tw Cen MT Condensed Extra Bold

TypoUpright BT

Ultra Condensed Sans 1

Ultra Condensed Sans 2

UNICORN

VAG Rounded Light **

VAG Rounded Thin **

Vagabond

Valiant

VARSITY

Verdana

Vogue

Westminster

Whimsy ICG

Whimsy ICG Heavy

Willow

Windsor BT

Windsor El BT

Windsor Lt BT

Windsor LtCn BT

Wonton ICG

Zelda

Zelda Italic

233